ALPHA
———

BOOKS ALSO BY DAWN BATES

Becoming Annie – The Biography of a Curious Woman (2020)

The Trilogy of Life Itself:

Friday Bridge – Becoming a Muslim, Becoming Everyone's Business (2nd Edition, 2017)

Walaahi – A firsthand account of living through the Egyptian Uprising and why I walked away from Islaam (2017)

Crossing The Line – A Journey of Purpose and Self-Belief (2017)

The Sacral Series:

Moana – One Woman's Journey Back to Self (2020)

Leila – A Life Renewed One Canvas at a Time (2020)

Pandora – Melting the Ice – One Dive at a Time (2021)

ALSO PUBLISHED BY DAWN PUBLISHING

Becoming the Champion – V1 Awareness by Korey Carpenter (2020)

Unlocked – Discover Your Hidden Keys by Carmelle Crinnion (2020)

Break Down to Wake Up – Journey Beyond the Now by Jocelyn Bellows (2020)

Standing in Strength – Inspirational Stories of Power Unleashed by Laarni Mulvey (2021)

The Recipe – A US Marine's Mindset for Success by Jake Cosme (2021)

The Democ'Chu Series by Nath Brye:

Slave Boy – Book 1 (2020)

Blood Child – Book 2 (2021)

ALPHA

SAVING HUMANITY ONE VAGINA AT A TIME

DAWN BATES

DAWN PUBLISHING

© 2021 Dawn Bates

Published by Dawn Publishing
www.dawnbates.com
The moral right of the author has been asserted.

For quantity sales or media enquiries, please contact the publisher at the website address above.

Cataloguing-in-Publication entry is available from the British Library.

ISBN: 978-1-913973-14-8 (paperback)
978-1-913973-15-5 (ebook)

Book cover design – Jerry Lampson
Publishing Consultant – Linda Diggle

All rights reserved. No part of this book may be reproduced, stored in a retrieval system, communicated or transmitted in any form or by means without written permission. All inquiries should be made to the publisher at the above address.

Disclaimer: The material in this publication is of the nature of general comment only and does not represent professional advice. It is not intended to provide specific guidance for particular circumstances and should not be relied on as the basis for any decision to take action or not to take action on any matters which it covers.

CONTENTS

Foreword	xi
Preface	xv
1. Getting acquainted	1
2. Understanding Culture	15
3. Freedom and movement	27
4. Reflections in the Mud	41
5. Silence Promotes Violence	53
6. Cuts of Purity	65
7. Risking it all for peanuts	75
8. The Chosen One	87
Cliterature	101
Gratitude	109
About Hajah Kandeh	113
About Dawn Bates	115
Also by Dawn Bates	117

Dedicated to
Women and their vaginas the world over who are taking a stand for their right to be whole.

FOREWORD

From the moment I heard her speak, I knew I was in the presence of someone who was going to make history.

What I didn't know, was that I would be blessed to be a part of it. I met Dawn through a group of incredible women in an online class where even the unnaturalness of a Zoom screen did not succeed in diminishing her radiance.

From the moment she opened her mouth and said the words "difficult stories" I knew I had to talk to her. I have lived one of those difficult stories.

We talked. It was as if I had known her all my life. I also hoped that somehow I would remain connected to someone who was so clear about their purpose. It was very humbling and scary to have been chosen to write the foreword for what I consider to be amongst the most important work of our time.

Dawn has made it her mission to go to those dark, forbidden places where no one dares to go, to see those things no one wants to look at, to tell truths we can no longer afford to bury. She is a light.

There are defining moments in every generation's history. This is ours.

We must keep in mind the movements of our collective histories, from the ancient to the contemporary.

Across time and continents, and in every nation, we will find human beings just like Dawn Bates who refuse to bow down to fear and tyranny, who understand that they have no other choice than to stand against oppression, even if the oppressors are our very own bed mates and those in charge, those we trust.

It is said that the true health and success of a society is directly related to the health and safety of its women, children, and elders. If the most at-risk members of a society are not considered as equal and deserving of the same rights, what is that society saying about itself?

We must consider that in Sierra Leone, my country of birth, nine out of ten children are abused before reaching puberty. We must also consider that globally, 1.2 million children are trafficked every year, and another 1.7 billion children experience some form of abuse over the course of a year; when we consider that there are 200 million women in the world who have suffered FGM (Female Genital Mutilation) and that an estimated 736 million have experienced intimate partner violence – sexual and otherwise – each year, we come to the cruel realisation that the class of people who need the most protection are those granted it the least.

Perhaps the hardest part to consider when looking at FGM is that it bears no benefits for the female victims whatsoever, and is purely for the convenience, physical and psychological comfort of men.

This is not a feminist manifesto. It is a human one.

Tradition should never trump our humanity.

Culture should never be an excuse for robbing children of their childhood.

Arranged marriages, female mutilation, child slavery, child labour, human trafficking, all speak of a world that has lost its way.

Having experienced violence in all these forms which I chronicle in my memoir *Daughter of a Thousand Stars*, I have earned the right to shout from the rooftops of every country and every nation that until, and unless society takes a stand against these atrocities that rob women of their right to a whole and fulfilling life, we will continue to see the decline in all things moral and just, in all things holy and beautiful.

And sadly, that society would have failed to secure the successful continuity of future generations.

As bleak as this picture looks, let us know that victory is inevitable; for victory begins the very second we decide to resist. Because, buried deep in our souls is the knowledge that we are connected, and that when one suffers, we all suffer.

The 2020 global pandemic has shown us this truism.

Imagine a world in which our governments and leaders prioritise the protection of women and children with the same urgency and resources that they prioritise economic growth and military strength!

We are planting trees to counter climate change. We are building new cars that are better for the environment.

We are taking steps to create a more just economy by raising the minimum wage. We most definitely can pass legislation that ensures the safety of its most vulnerable.

I did not choose the circumstances of my life but I can choose how I use the gift of my voice to tell my story and join in the chorus of brave, strong warrior women and men to say "enough".

A lone voice may go unheard but with the unbeatable power in the collective, we can and will reclaim the sacred lives of women and children in every corner of the globe.

This book, and others like it, will be our gift to humanity and our future generations.

Hajah Kandeh,
Author and Women's Rights Advocate

PREFACE

This book has been incredibly challenging to write. It was a story gifted to me fifteen years prior to writing this book, and upon writing the first chapter my body reacted in such a way I got acquainted with the porcelain in the hotel bathroom where I was staying, and cried an incredible amount of tears.

The books in *The Sacral Series* may not be easy to read for many people, but they are also not easy to write. Choosing which parts of the story to share, making sure I protect identities and families, all whilst honouring the various cultures, faiths and the people on the periphery of the stories who have been of support to the individuals who trusted me with their stories provides me with a challenge like no other I have had as a writer.

As an author it is an honour and a privilege to be gifted a story to write, and it is also a duty in many ways to be able to put my gift as a writer into practice to bring awareness of situations around the world which need addressing, and in bringing them to an end.

I do not expect there to be an end to the many things I have written about in this book, or any of the books I write, just because I have written about them. The complexities of the situations are just that, complex; and it will take generations for many of the practices you will read about in this book to come to an end.

It will also take a huge amount of courage for women – and the men who love them – to take a stand against some deeply evil and misguided individuals and organisations, not forgetting the courage it will take for them to take a stand against their families, their culture and their faiths for the practices in this book to stop.

As a white, western woman some may wonder why I am the one who is sharing this story, but this is not just an African problem, this is a humanity problem. My readers span the globe and transcend cultures, faiths and nations. So sharing this story, and others within *The Sacral Series*, more people become aware of the situations, giving a voice to the voiceless and an even louder voice to those screaming to be heard.

And they are screaming. In pain, in hope, in desperation and in some cases the relief of victory at being heard by someone outside of their communities.

The subtitle 'Saving humanity one vagina at a time' is a bold statement, but if this book wakes up just one person who takes one action, which stops one woman being violated either by FGM (Female Genital Mutilation) or rape within their own marriage, African or Western, Asian or Latino, Australasian or Russian, then this statement stands true in its boldness.

We can save humanity one vagina at a time, through education, through awareness, through courage and through solidarity as women, as men and as humans.

The question is, once you have read this book, what will you do with what you learn?

ONE

GETTING ACQUAINTED

Mingling in the foyer over teas and coffees, women were either in shock or so fired up they could have charged the university for a month on kinaesthetic energy. From the quiet words of disbelief featuring statements such as "What some of those women go through" to the pure anger of "Evil bastards, the lot of them" it was hard to know where to stand amongst them all. So I stood back and just watched, listened and learned.

"You don't want to join in the conversations?" said a strong voice from my right hand side.

"Not really," I answered.

"Why not?" asked the beautiful black African woman standing beside me.

"Because it's all middle class, *Guardian* readers who came for the shock factor and the sense they want to do something, but will never do anything, if you want my honest answer," I replied.

"Nice to meet you, my name is Al," she said, holding out her hand to shake mine. "That's a very interesting point of view by the way, and one I can imagine doesn't make you very popular."

"It doesn't, but like they say, the truth will at first piss you off, but then it will set you free... if you let it. My name is Moana, nice to meet you too Al, although I know Al is not your real name, not with your Angolan heritage."

"How did you know I was Angolan?" Al replied looking at me with a frown.

"Your accent, it is the same as a friend of mine. How long have you been here in England?" I asked.

"I've been here for about eight years now, five legally you could say. I have seen you before, wanted to speak with you on a few occasions, but you never stick around very long after the lectures or speeches have been given. Why?"

"Really? You've seen me before? Hmmm, where? And no, I don't, because like I said, most of them here want to be seen to be seen, rather than putting skin in the game and actually doing something to make the changes needed in the world."

She laughed at me. "I like you. And yes, I have seen you quite a few times, heard some of your talks and debates. You're not very English are you," she stated rather than asked.

"You don't know me well enough to know whether you like me or not," I laughed. "And you wouldn't be the first to say that about me. So, what did you think of the lecture?"

"Honestly? I thought the awareness it has raised has been valuable, but like you, I know most of these people in attendance will only be using the fact they have attended as a prestige thing or for a sense of looking intelligent and educated at a dinner party. Very few will get involved in the organisations who are doing the work on the ground to save these young girls, and very few will go to Africa or the 'ethnic parts of town' and get their hands dirty because they wouldn't be able to sleep at night if they knew the true extent of the problem. Like you say, 'middle class *Guardian* readers' – most are all the same," she stated with conviction. "What are your plans now? Are you staying for the Q&A?"

"Oh, I'm staying. I've got questions I want to ask," I replied with a mischievous giggle.

"How did I know you were going to say that?" said Al laughing out loud. "And Al is short for Alpha, a name Angolan society will remember for a long time to come. Now let's go sit in and cause hell in the Q&A, then if you are free afterwards, we are going out for dinner."

"It's a date!" I smiled.

We walked together back into the lecture theatre, and I saw another friend Jack who was sat towards the back of the room. He shook his head and laughed to himself. He knew what was coming, and when I saw Alpha acknowledge him too, I laughed. "You know him too?"

"Oh yes, he was one of the first people I met when I came here to Sheffield. Has encouraged me in many ways and helped me with the movement back home in Angola. How do you know him?"

"Oh you know, a project here and there," I replied. "Let's just say we have gotten up to mischief together a few times politically, upsetting a few people here and there, and an apple cart or two."

"Those blasted apples, always getting us women into trouble," she laughed.

At this point I just couldn't help but laugh loudly, much to the disgrace of the said female *Guardian* readers we had avoided in the foyer. "You know, if us laughing offends them, then that just says so much in confirming what we were saying a few moments ago," commented Alpha.

"Hmm mmm… but then we may just be making all that up, you know us humans are meaning making machines…"

"Oh very tactful…" laughed Alpha.

I had a feeling this woman I had only just met would be a great friend, and my mind was spinning with ideas on how we could work together. Here we were at a university lecture on female genital mutilation (FGM) and child bride selection in Africa and we were laughing together, making similar assumptions about the others who were here in the room, and discovering we knew the same people; people who like us, knew that to deal with the horrors this lecture was about, we needed to release the traumatic images and information we had just been given, confirming a lot of what we already knew, and introducing us to new organisations on the ground in the various African countries, from the north in Morocco all the way down to Zimbabwe and Johannesburg.

After the welcome back from the break was done and the expert panel was introduced, the questions began.

We were told that more than 200 million girls and women alive have been 'cut' in thirty countries, and that FGM was mostly carried out on young girls either in infancy, and most certainly before the age of 15 when they were being selected for marriage by men as old as their father.

Alpha's hand went up, "Why is it that you are saying Africa and the Middle East when the Middle East is in Africa?"

The speaker, a Human Rights Advocate from the UK, blushed stumbled and then gathered herself saying, "This is how we distinguish them politically, and helps us gather data."

"Yes, but why are you distinguishing politically in this way? The girls in the Middle East are African, so unless you are trying to distinguish between them on religious grounds, which is what I am assuming you are doing because it fits political agendas and funding for your work, then you need to state this, and then go on to state that FGM has no foundation in either Islam or Christianity."

FUCK YES! Were the words that went through my mind and a rapturous round of applause spread throughout the auditorium. I liked this woman! A LOT. So did many of the women in the audience and the energy in the room changed. It was like the herd of elephants in the room had just found a watering hole elsewhere to drink from.

"I do understand your point and I thank you for raising it. I would like to reassure you that I do not do this work for funding purposes only, and it is something I deeply care about putting a stop to," replied the speaker with her perfectly nuanced political training in the art of public speaking.

"Why do you do this work then?" asked another lady from the other side of the room. Everyone turned to her and waited for the follow up. "Because, no disrespect to you and the other ladies here in the room from the UK and the rest of Europe, but this is not an English problem, so what is it to you?"

"I disagree," said the speaker. "This is very much an English problem, as it is also an American problem, a French problem and any other nation that has a woman as a civilian. This is a female problem that transcends any nationality, faith and culture."

"Ooo good answer," whispered Alpha, either to herself or to me, I wasn't quite sure.

I agreed. "We need to speak with her afterwards, depending on what she says next."

"Hmm mmm, if only to educate her on what is an African."

"As women, we have long been abused at the hands of men, tortured for simply being women, objectified and celebrated for our beauty as well as punished and hidden away for something we have no control over. When any female has her right to choose taken away from her, we all have our rights taken away. This is not an African problem…" she said looking at Alpha. "Nor is it an Asian problem, and by Asian I make the point of stating South Asian as it is not reported in Far East Asia or North Asia. We are women and if we are going to bring an end to this tradition of removing the external genitalia of females then we need to join together and drop the idea that the white Western woman has no part to play in finding a solution to this dreadful crime against the females of the world.

"Not only is this a violation of the human rights of

girls and women, but it is used as emotional and mental abuse, ostracising and excluding young girls and women from communities which leads in some cases to being beaten to death and left homeless on the streets of their country because they are considered impure."

The man to her right then spoke up. "It is also a huge financial burden for twenty seven of those thirty countries it is most common in because the problems these women have when it comes to urinating, cysts, infections and in some cases reconstructive surgery due to tribal leaders or unlicensed doctors performing this terrible act upon these young girls, runs into $1.4 billon US dollars per year."

"So is this a financial problem for you then, sir? And what about you, ma'am? You never got a chance to answer why you do this work." Questions came from a few rows behind me.

The female speaker answered before the male speaker had a chance. "I do this work because I may be white, and English, but I grew up in South Africa and a friend of mine was subjected to FGM when she was just nine years of age. Both she and her baby died during childbirth due to the damage done to the insides of her vagina as a child. That is why I do this work, in honour of her, so if there are any more judgements any of you would like to make, then I suggest we get them out of the way now and move on with what this conference is really about, and that is how we can make a real difference instead of just gathering knowledge to look good at dinner parties."

The emotion within her was more than obvious, and the painful memories of her friend were felt by many.

"Well, she just called out the *Guardian* readers in the room!" whispered Alpha.

"Hmm didn't she just," I replied looking over at a group of women who were a few rows in front of us to the left, who were now looking really rather uncomfortable. I didn't have to say anything to Alpha, she had clocked them as well, as had many others in the room. The ladies were the focal point of many, and I felt for them as we have all judged them, rightly or wrongly. I wanted to break the ice which had fallen over the room and so raised my hand.

"Picking up on the end of your last sentence, I know many of the 'dinner party conversational types' who just come along and learn about this kind of topic so they can discuss it at dinner, but isn't the fact that the 'dinner party types' are here still part of raising awareness? Because they themselves may not be in a position to help, but their fellow guests at dinner parties may be?"

All eyes turned on me.

A question came from several rows back, "Moana you are not one of those types so why are you making it look like you are defending yourself?" As I turned I saw another friend I had not seen during the initial lecture nor during the comfort break.

"Well, as you know from business networking Anwar, it is not always the people in the room that you do business with, and this is no different. Those who are here in the audience are still being made aware of the situation, and I am guessing from the conversations I overheard during the comfort break that at least 35% of the people in this room were hearing about it properly for the first time. You then have about another 40% who were deepening their knowledge on the subject, myself included. So I would say that's, what, about eighty people? And at the average dinner party there are eight guests, so just doing some simple maths of eight times eighty that's six hundred and forty people that will now have a better understanding of the subject, and if we use the rule of four, six hundred and forty times four that's what?... Two thousand four hundred and sixty people who will be aware of the situation by the end of the week. So does it matter that this room is made up of the diehard activists, the researchers, the community leaders and *The Guardian* reader dinner party guests? I say no, it doesn't."

Anwar smiled at me with a 'well played' look on his face, and I looked at him knowing he had set me up, the bloody git! There was also a round of applause, and Alpha just sat looking at me. "Well hot dang lady! That was impressive!"

"What, the quick maths?" I laughed back at her.

"No. Pulling those ladies out of a judgemental shit heap and doing it with style. And I take it you know Anwar then?"

"Oh my days! Is there anyone else here we both know that we have to have words with for not introducing us before?" I chuckled.

"I think you raise an excellent point Moana, and my apologies to those in the audience who felt the judgement from me. You demonstrated why these events are so vital, not just for FGM and child bride selections, but also for a whole range of subjects which really do need addressing. I will pass over to my esteemed colleague now for him to answer the question." She sat down and nodded in my direction, and then looked back at Anwar and smiled.

I turned around to Anwar who nodded at me, and I knew he was drawing me out in his unique style of introductions. I was *so* going to have words with him after this event.

As the event continued and the four speakers dealt with question after question, many of which I wanted to also ask, such as the selection process of brides being almost like a business between doctors, priests, imams and the men of the various countries where FGM and child brides were prevalent.

It transpired that doctors who had the better practices were sending lists of names to the influential businessmen of the towns and cities, whilst the poorer doctors were also sending names to prevent their practices from being shut to the local elders. These girls were being selected as soon as they turned up at the clinics and sold off to the highest bidder, and the parents of the girls thought nothing of it because it is what has always happened and it is just part of their everyday lives. Parents would even drop clues to the doctors, priests and imams about the kind of husband they wanted their daughters to marry. These little girls stood no chance of escaping the blade and enjoying a pleasurable sex life, but that is why the men did it, so they were secure in the knowledge that their bride wouldn't go looking for sex elsewhere. A man's insecurity used to create a solution for themselves whilst destroying the lives of these young girls and women, in many ways.

Parents knew if their daughter had not been cut early, then the chances of her 'being promised' to a suitable husband was slim, so in some places there was almost a race to the clinic amongst the families to get their daughter cut as early as possible. Strangely, my thoughts went to the fact that parents pierced their daughters ears at birth so she looked pretty in photos, taking away their daughters choice of having holes in their bodies. They may be two extremes of physical abuse and violation of choice, with vastly different outcomes but cutting off a clitoris and punching holes into a baby's body was still violating the body and taking away choice. Tears sprung to my eyes. I had circumcised both my boys, so I wasn't much better. I had abused my boys and taken away their right to choose whether to keep their foreskin.

I raised my hand. "Sitting here I have just been hit with the realisation that as a mother I am no different really to the parents who circumcise their girls. Why? Because I had my boys circumcised in the belief that it was cleaner and would give them more pleasure, or at least that is how I reasoned it when my husband said it was the thing to do in Islaam. I relented for religious reasons as well as believing it was cleaner and the more pleasure aspect. But it doesn't make it right what I did, or any different, does it?"

The room fell silent. There were many Muslims and Jews in the audience so I knew that the men were either circumcised or the mothers and fathers in the room of these two faiths had circumcised their sons. We were all guilty of violating our children and taking away their right to choose. A deeply reflective mood fell over everyone.

"Well that killed the mood," whispered Alpha into my ear.

"Yeah, well… it needed saying," I replied.

"I can see what Moana has just said has had an impact on us all," Alpha declared to the room. "And she's right in many ways, those of us who circumcise our boys for religious reasons, as well as cleanliness and increased pleasure, are guilty of violating our child's body and taking away their choice, but the intention of circumcision is different. We are not taking something away from our boys with the intention of depriving them pleasure and getting them married off to the highest bidder; nor are we trying to control them through fear of marriage at an early age, which as we know is akin to these little girls being raped." She looked at me, put her hand on my hand and said, "I know this is a painful realisation for you, but you cannot put yourself in the same category as these men who mutilate, rape and control these girls and their families. As a survivor of this torture, I have had many problems over the years with cysts, incredibly painful sex, and difficulty trusting a man. Our boys do not have these long term effects due to having their foreskin taken away. Ask any man who has been circumcised later in his life due to converting to Islaam and he will tell you that sex is more pleasurable afterwards. So if anything, you've done your boys a favour."

"That she 'as," said a male voice from the other side of the lecture hall. "And this is probably an over share, so forgive me if you will, but I had an infection a few years ago and had to have my foreskin removed. It wasn't for religious reasons at all, but I'll tell ya now, I'm a lot bloody 'appier in the bedroom since. I feel everything!" he laughed.

The room broke out in laughter with him. Some laughs

were out of modesty, some were due to the over share, and others were just laughing in celebration with him.

Professor Costa stood up, "Well on that note ladies and gentlemen, I think that brings the event to a pleasant end."

"Well that bloke certainly thinks the end is pleasant now," giggled Alpha.

"Alpha!" I giggled back.

Thanks were given to all the speakers, all those who had asked questions, and we were gifted information packs on our way out.

"Well that turned out to be a good event. I do like these events you know, and so glad they open them up to the public," Alpha stated as she put her arm through mine and told me I was going home with her for dinner.

I didn't have to be back by a particular time as I didn't really know what time the event would wrap up so had hired a babysitter for the whole evening. I loved to chat at the end of these events with those in attendance, so me going back to Alpha's for dinner was not different to me staying behind for a chat and a networking session.

"I just want to say bye to Anwar and Jack before we leave," I said.

"Oh don't bother, they are coming for dinner as well, so is Professor Costa and the speakers," she responded.

"Oh well then, I'll just go to the loo and meet you in the foyer," I said heading off in the direction of the toilets.

TWO
UNDERSTANDING CULTURE

Arriving at Alpha's home was a sensory delight. Colours of Africa everywhere in tapestries, paints and cushions of light blues, terracotta and vivid sunburnt yellow. Homemade candles with nutmeg and clove danced with the smells of the food already cooking in the oven. The closer I got to the kitchen I could smell the cardamom and cumin chicken, boiled rice, and garlic vegetables and took in a deep breath narrating all the smells I could smell. My tummy rumbled and I was more than ready to eat whatever was served for dinner… well, other than the infamous insect soup, which I was sure she wasn't going to serve.

"Someone looks and sounds hungry," she smiled at me as she arranged the cushions on the floor for us all to sit and enjoy our meal. "You know how to ball up your rice I am sure?" she stated as a question.

"I do indeed! But will still want a spoon for that soup you've got on the stove. What is it? Smells like lentil and okra with a tonne of garlic," I replied.

"Do you know how African you are? It is like our culture is embedded deep in your DNA woman!"

"Well, food is my favourite ingredient and I make sure I know what I am eating when eating new dishes... and, like you, I combine the foods from around the world because, let's face it, lentil and okra soup isn't very traditionally Angolan from what I know... even though the ingredients are. And you know, we are all connected, all born of one another. I am no less African than you are English. I'm also very hungry, so on sensory overload with this delicious food you are gifting us."

"There are some caramelised peanuts in honey in a bowl in the sitting room, you can nibble on those if you want whilst we wait for Jack, Anwar and whoever else turns up."

"Hmm caramelised nuts.... yum! So.... you said you have been in the UK for eight years and Jack has helped you with the social movement, which I am not surprised about to be honest. He pretends to be all corporate but he is a proper community activist. He's like one of those stealth ninjas, and Anwar... he's a cheeky sod!"

Alpha laughed. "Oh the way he set you up with that speaker, that was a classic move on his part!"

"I know right! And I walked right into it! Ooo, I think that is them now. Did you want me to get the door whilst you finish the dinner setting?"

"Yes please," she said returning to the kitchen for glasses and plates.

The night rolled on and there was laughter as we all told stories of how we knew each other, and the escapades which followed. Alpha had met Jack at a Black Minority and Ethnic (BME) community networking event hosted by one of the local business support agencies. He had been impressed with her fierce energy and deep belly laugh. They had worked together on some of the regeneration projects for the BME community ever since with Alpha speaking at events, raising awareness of what it meant to be a recent resident, and how to integrate rather than isolate yourself. There were projects they had worked on which had crossed many of the ones he and I had worked on, and both Alpha and I told him off for not introducing us to each other before.

"I wasn't sure if I was ready for you two to meet, let alone the world being ready!" he joked. "The important thing is, now you two know each other, what are you going to create together?"

"And don't tell us you haven't already thought about it yet either," added Anwar. "We know you both too well to know that you have already been running through all the projects you are working on and how you both fit into each other's plans."

Alpha let out a raucous laugh, one that could only come from someone who has experienced such deep trauma and risen above the victim story to create greatness and not allow the world to keep her small. I knew a lot about the poverty which has intensified over the last few decades since the civil war had started back in 1975 thanks to a friend of mine and the research I had done since meeting him.

I had found out that when Angolans started reclaiming their independence from the Portuguese, which ended in a bloodless coup in Portugal after thirteen years of bitter fighting in the War of Independence, the Angolans then descended into yet another war. This one created devastation on many levels due to the increased international and domestic pressures of the People's Movement for the Liberation of Angola (MPLA), which was formed back in 1956 by The Portuguese Communist Party and supported by the Eastern Bloc countries. The National Union for the Total Independence of Angola (UNITA) consisted largely of the Ovimbundu of central Angola, and I discovered the Ovimbundu were the country's largest ethnic group at thirty-seven percent of the population and UNITA was given the backing by the US and South Africa. My curiosity peaked.

This was not about independence of a people this was about getting rich and having control over certain aspects of the society. It didn't take me long to figure out it had to do with blood diamonds, or rather the more palatable term 'conflict diamonds'.

As with all African wars, the support offered always came from the white Westerners' who kept conflicts going for as long as the country had minerals, oils and items of financial gain. In Angola's case it was all three of the most expensive items: diamonds, oil and people.

It was no surprise that the US, South Africa, and the Soviet Union got involved considering the minerals and oil which lay under the earth. The race for the diamonds was the biggest contributing factor in all the African countries, although that was not the narrative put out in the mass media. It was no secret to those who dug beneath the surface that every civil war in Africa, whether it was Sierra Leone, Liberia, Cote d'Ivoire, the Republic or Democratic

Republic of Congo or the Central African Republic, including Angola was funded by conflict diamonds.

Cuba's revolutionary leader Fidel Castro got involved by sending his own troops to Angola, because being an educated man, he knew the Portuguese had gone to Angola seeking gold, and then started trading in humans with the slave trade, just like they had with Brazil, Angola's colonial sister. Of all the places Castro had sent his armies to support countries in their fight for freedom, Angola would feel the Cuban presence the most.

After we had feasted on the delicious food Alpha served us and gotten cosy on the cushions with some cardamom tea, I had to call out the elephant in the room. "Okay, so I know a bit about the history of Angola, the War of Independence and the civil war, but not much… and I may be making stuff up here, but I am guessing you are either in exile, unable to return to Angola or you are just choosing to be here in the UK because you can gain more support for your movement, which you have still not told me about."

"You would be correct in thinking I am in exile, and that me being here will also give support to my movement back home in Africa. This is why Jack here has been helping, to access the information I needed to make me a British citizen, but also to help me figure out how to keep the movement alive in Angola, Namibia, Zambia and the Congo. You see the movement may have started with me in Angola, but we women started to look at our country's independence in a way that the men never saw coming." She looked over at Jack as if at this point he was used to picking up the story, but he remained silent.

"Freedom and independence, once it appears on your horizon, even if all seems hopeless with the men shooting at each other, takes many forms. Whilst we wanted our independence from the Portuguese, and the men went about shooting each other, there were a few women who wanted a different kind of independence. The political conflict created a storm within us women which once it had arrived could never go out. We may not have been on the battlefield, but there were battles raging within us, bringing uncertainty about parts of our culture to the fore, making us rethink who we were and what we wanted moving forward. Those of us who dared to speak against our tribes, our people, our elders, and the religious leaders soon become a threat to them, and we sparked something within other women, and although we were scared, we could not put that spark out. It was a fire that never went out."

"Beautifully said Alpha," piped up Anwar. "You see Moana, this is a problem which affects all African countries from the North in Morocco and Algeria to the southernmost part of South Africa. The health problems we are seeing here in our own city with women and young girls from South Asian communities, and those from Indonesia are increasingly alarming. I know you understand this is a global situation, and that it is fuelling the undercurrent of racism and prejudice within many European countries due to the influx of Arab and African refugees, so this is one of the reasons I believe you two have come together to make a difference. Bridging the gap between it being a foreign problem to a global problem. Alpha's movement, although it started back in the dirt tracks of almost twenty years ago, needs a new voice. You understand Islaam and the Arab world better than most English women ever will, and we need you to make sure the world knows it isn't just an Islaamic problem, or an African problem, but a humanity problem."

"First of all Anwar, thank you for recognising my understanding of the Islaamic faith and the Arab world, but I am not sure how much I can commit to this movement. Abdu is away, so I am taking care of the boys on my own, I have my businesses to sort out and you know I am also moving to Egypt. All that said, you know I will always support movements like this in any way I can. I do need to have more details on the movement though, and so far I don't really know much about it, other than I am looking at a woman who has been through what I can only imagine to be a lot of trauma personally and politically. I need to know who and what I am dealing with, how much has been achieved so far and what the KPIs are for the future of the movement. Who else is involved and what alliances have fallen through and why. Once I understand all of this, then I will be in a much better position to know how I can help and how much time I can commit to the project," I responded whilst my mind was racing with the fact that moving to Egypt might just be the right time to learn more about FGM in the Arab world. I knew it happened there in the more remote towns outside of Cairo and Alexandria, but just how deep it ran would be a project all by itself.

Jack responded to me. "Well, why not meet up next week ladies, you can learn about Alpha's story, and then the three of us can meet with the team at the Asylum and

Refugee Council. You remember Tracy, Moana? She was there when we ran the project with the Palestinians a few years ago. I also think it would be a good idea for us to have Dr Costa join us, the one who led the lecture this afternoon."

"I agree," said Anwar.

"Now hang on a second gentlemen," motioned Alpha. "Before we start running away with who we are and are not going to be meeting with next week, Moana needs to know the full story, and as this is my home, and she is my guest, I request that we respect that her and I have only just met, although it feels as though we have been friends for more than this lifetime. I request that one of you gentlemen take her home and I will call her tomorrow to arrange another meeting of minds. How does that sound to you Moana?"

"That sounds like a better idea, because it is getting late and the boys will be in bed already, so I will have missed saying goodnight and reading to them. Let me just give them a call, just in case," I said as I stood up to stretch my legs and retrieve my phone from my bag.

The men helped Alpha take the things into the kitchen whilst she packed away the leftover food into Tupperware boxes for my boys to enjoy their new Aunty's cooking. Watching whilst I was speaking with Chloe on the phone, the young woman who was looking after the boys, I enjoyed watching the culture exchanges happening. Jordanian, Angolan and English dancing with the dynamics of gender, and it working perfectly together.

"Thanks Chloe, I'll be back in about half an hour," I said ending the call.

"Right, so here is food for my new nephews, and tell them Aunty Alpha will come by and see them one day soon," she said to me, whilst turning to Jack and Anwar. "Make sure you get her home in one piece Jack and give my salaams to your wife Anwar. Tell her I will see her for coffee soon. Now go on all of you and let this old woman rest. All this talk has left me tired."

"Old woman my arse," quipped Jack. "You will outlive us all!"

"Now that wouldn't be any fun at all, if you die before me, I will have only the bastards in Angola to haunt for what they did to me. I will need some light-hearted haunting too, to break up the heavier kind," threatened Alpha with yet more humour in her voice. She really was remarkable in the way that she radiated such peace within, joked about those who obviously tortured her to some degree and was powerful in her feminine essence. We embraced like old friends saying our goodbyes, then men both saluted her, something I had not seen either of them do to anyone else before, even though we had all worked together on many projects in and around the region before.

I was now even more intrigued about Alpha's story, and the scars on the back of her neck and across the front of her forearms, scars that she was not afraid to show. She not only intrigued me, but had inspired me with the projects her, Jack and Anwar had worked on. I was also puzzled about why she had not approached me before if she had seen me at previous events. She just didn't seem to be the kind of woman to shy away from approaching someone. On my way home Jack and I caught up on what he had been working on, and how his wife Sarah and the children were, and how this movement of Alpha's had impacted him and his wife, who was also an activist. He told me that she was deeply moved by Alpha's story and was working closely with a team of journalists from Birmingham, Amsterdam and Angola. I looked at him curiously and he noted the look on my face.

"All will become clear when you speak with Alpha," he smiled.

We arrived at my home, I thanked him for the ride and said, "See you next week then, and say hi to Sarah for me."

"Will do! Night Moana… and don't stay up all night researching FGM and Angola. Alpha will tell you all you need to know."

I laughed and replied, "You know me too well my friend, good night." And with that I turned and walked across my driveway into my home, only to hear the boys giggling upstairs. I took off my coat and called out to them, "Mummy's home! Who wants a story?"

"We do!" they cheered. The conflict of Angola's diamonds, FGM and politics fell away for another night whilst I read *Dr Seuss's Sleep Book* to my boys, slightly distracted by my comment in the lecture about their circumcision, which didn't last for long, especially when trying not to get tongue tied with the moose drinking moose juice and not goose juice, and the goose not drinking moose juice. Oh how I loved Dr Seuss and his brilliance with words, as did my boys, and in true English parenting style, it was storytime before sleep. I treasured these moments and after what I had heard in the lectures earlier on in the day, the thought of reading hundreds of children to sleep each night with Dr Seuss brought a smile to my face and warm fuzzies to my heart.

How anyone could hurt a child was beyond me, let alone torture and rape them. Knowing many parents arranged it all, often out of the normalcy of it all, and sometimes out of fear of starving or being tortured themselves was even more heart breaking.

I kissed my boys goodnight, told them I loved them, and stood and watched them sleep for what felt like a few moments. Angels, the pair of them.

Making my way down the stairs to make a cup of tea and finish off my day, my mind went out to the parents who were becoming aware of what they were actually doing to their daughters. The turmoil they must be going through, because as Alpha had said earlier on in the evening, once you are shown something and that spark is lit, it ignites many things within you that you just cannot put out. I sent the parents around the world who needed it courage and strength to speak up and out. As parents we needed to step up for our children, and the children of others, because it really does take a community to raise children.

THREE

FREEDOM AND MOVEMENT

"Where are we going?" I asked as Alpha pulled up in her car to collect me.

"Out into nature, what we are to talk about is going to need nature in abundance and the freedom to speak without upsetting or offending others nearby. Do you have any preferences?"

"Well we don't actually have to go anywhere, I have a large garden, but if you do wish to go somewhere, let's head out to Lady Bower, up Manchester Road," I offered.

"I was thinking Lady Bower, so let's go there. I haven't been for a while and it has everything – water, tress and sheep… so that is a perfect choice," she agreed.

"Sheep?" I queried.

"Yes, I love eating lamb, so they make me hungry and after this we are going to want to eat," she said in all seriousness.

I couldn't help but laugh my head off. "Oh you do make me laugh!"

"Oh I am deadly serious. Lamb is my favourite

ingredient. I had never had it until I came to the UK and now… well let's just say I have collected many recipes. And they are cute, especially the little ones when they jump about as if they have springs in their feet."

We headed off up the road, music on and I couldn't help but look at this larger than life Angolan woman singing along to Ed Sheeran as though she was at a sell out concert at Wembley.

"You know we African's are loud and proud people, and I know what you are thinking. You are confused first of all at my music choice, but this young man is so sexy with his shyness, red hair and freckles. And you know when we Africans sing, which we always do, we SING!" Alpha said moving her body with the rhythm of the music and her energy was so captivating.

"You are so happy and energised. It is beautiful to experience."

"Why thank you darling! I am just grateful every day to be alive and free, so whilst I am alive, I am going to be free in every and any way possible. Life is a gift, and when you have seen and experienced what I have seen and experienced, you don't take life for granted in any way shape or form. You English folks think you are free, but you are the most uptight nation I have ever come across. Admittedly I haven't been to many countries in the West, and I hear the German's are more uptight, but that is from the English and the history between the two of you doesn't leave much room for a non-biased opinion. The thing is you think you are free, but you are so worried about looking good, being proper and showing you are free, that you are trapped by the very essence of proving you are free. If you were truly free you would not have to prove you are free. Freedom is a state of being my darling, not a point to prove. Now sing with me."

We sang our hearts out, and garnered looks from passing motorists, but neither of us cared. I had sung and danced in my car ever since I had learnt to drive. I had learnt that from my mum and dad. They were always singing in the car, and I hoped that my boys would carry on the 'family tradition' and pass it onto their children. Singing was a great way of expressing ourselves and releasing any residual energy that lingered in your body, and with what I could only begin to imagine was about to be shared with me, this singing was going to be an essential way of Alpha preparing herself to share her story with me.

"So where would you like me to start?" she asked me as we started our walk.

"I think maybe the movement, and then work backwards that way I can understand where you are at with the movement and then you can build upon they why behind it all. It will also give us chance to brace ourselves for some of the heavier content of this conversation and ensure we are deeper into the open space, because I have a feeling we are going to need to see off into the distance and be far away from others."

"Good idea, and well perceived my darling," she said looping her arm in mine as we set off up the trail into the wide open spaces. "So, this movement, it is multifaceted and has many different arms you could say, like an octopus, except with three arms. We have the educational side of it, the political and the medical. Under each of those we have another three aspects.

"The education is focused on educating the people of Angola primarily as that is where I started all this. From there it is easy for us to spread the message far and wide. Then we have the education of the elders, the doctors and of course the women themselves. The third arm of this is to educate the rest of the world about what is going on, what has gone on and the ramifications for the future.

"Then we have the political aspects where we are lobbying the education ministers to provide resources to bring awareness of the dangers and human rights violations FGM and rape cause, educating the doctors and surgeons in how to deal with the effects of FGM, as well as lobbying to make sure the law makers bring justice to all those who do this without a medical license, and hopefully make it illegal to perform even without a medical license.

"The medical side of the movement is a mix of both of the above but runs deeper because we are making sure the physical, emotional, mental and financials of FGM are dealt with. It is not enough to simply treat the physical aftermath, but also the mental and emotional health. The financial aspect comes into it because, as I said the other night, many doctors are bribed by wealthy businessmen to find them a child bride who has a 'beautiful vagina cut cleanly' and so they hire the best doctors to find their bride. We have to do more at a government level for the doctors who refuse to take part in this practice to show them that there is another way to keep their medical practice and make it the better practice. So we educate these doctors, fund much of their training and sponsor equipment, which is invaluable to them. Money and power rules the African world more than the rest of the world in many ways because we have been poor for so long. If we can show the people that behaving honourably, and in line with human rights is going to win them prestige from the rest of the world then they will follow.

"The other aspect to the political point of view is to withdraw government contracts from these businessmen who take a child bride."

"Hitting them where it really hurts," I added.

"Exactly, but this is the biggest problem because the governments are funded by these men. The election campaigns, the social gatherings and the dinners are all sponsored by the big companies, and these are the men that not only buy these brides but traffic them between each other as sex slaves. It is a big problem, and we see a lot of it happening with Portugal and Brazil. Many of our girls are shipped all over the world and reportedly gone missing or died from illness, supported by the doctors certificates which are forged by doctors who are paid a lot of money to stay silent. The movement has to be a three-pronged approach because without the education, we cannot have the people realise what is happening, so they do not challenge the government and the big companies and the medical companies have to be willing to treat this as a form of abuse rather than just a cultural tradition that has been going on for over 2000 years across the world.

"Did you know it was used amongst the high societies of England and the rest of Europe, by Gynaecologists to curb promiscuity which would bring shame on the families? And the more beautiful the labia the higher the dowry the family received?"

"I did not know that. Where did you find out about that?" I replied really surprised and yet not surprised at all.

"Well, when you do as much research as I have done over the years, it is one thread of information which leads to another which leads to another. I knew that the high societies in the Arab and Sub Saharan African countries used this practice to curb sexual desires and promiscuity, so I wondered where else this happened, asking myself where were women most promiscuous, and how were they controlled by society? As you know, when you ask smarter questions, you uncover more information. Asking the question 'Were women in England subjected to FGM?' would not bring the information I was seeking but asking 'How was sexual promiscuity curbed in European high society?' brought a whole lot more information, and when you know what you are looking for, and then ask about those 'medical practices' things start to unravel," Alpha stated.

"Okay, so you have this movement, and it is how many years old now?"

"It was seven years old at the end of February to mark the death of Jonas Savimbi, who, I am pretty sure you know was the revolutionary politician and rebel leader of the UNITA party. I thought it very fitting to launch it on the 22nd of February because, like you, I believe in Numerology, so I had chosen 222 as the launch date. It just happened to be the day Savimbi died… so not lucky for him, but lucky for many Angolans, some would say."

"And you? Do you believe he was a good man?" I asked.

"Well that is the biggest question of them all, because

when you know that he wanted to be a doctor, and he travelled overseas to study, you know he had both the desire to heal and to learn more about his trade. He wanted true independence for Angola, away from the Portuguese rule, and he was anti-communism. I believe he had good intentions, and I always believe he knew how to play the politics with the US and China. He was trained in medicine, politics and guerrilla warfare by the world best mentors and teachers, and I believe he was also conflicted. He knew that to save millions, the death of a few would be necessary. Do I think he was also a bad man? Yes I do, because to be so ruthless and succeed at the level he did, he had to betray himself, his family and his people to obtain the bigger agenda. I would never want to be a politician, or a political leader at his level because I do not have it in me to make the kind of choices he had to make to stay in favour. Having my own movement has challenged me many times, and I have always had to come back to prayer and ask for guidance because I know I have to do what is right by all."

"The greatest happiness of the greatest number. Hume and Utilitarianism, interesting philosophy that one, and one that I don't agree with to be honest."

"And why is that?" asked Alpha.

"Because by making sure you have the greatest happiness of the greatest number means you are giving in to sheeple and dumbing down nations because most people don't want to think or act in the greatest way for all. They want the easiest most convenient route, so the greatest happiness doesn't always bring about the right moral answer," I replied.

"I get that, and that is why I, and I would assume Savimbi and other political leaders, find it really quite tough being a leader."

"So, back to your movement, you said it was set up seven years ago, I am guessing that was officially, but before then it would have been grassroots and you raising hell with protests, leaflets and speaking out at women's events etc?"

"You do like to get down to business, don't you? Jack said you did, and Anwar warned me that you would cut to the chase," laughed Alpha.

"Well it is important we do get down to it, I have to be back in the city to collect the boys from school at 5:30 pm. I put them into after school care as I thought we may take all day. They were happy about it as the get to play board games with their friends, and they haven't been in after-school care for a while, so all good. So… officially seven years going? And who is helping you?" I asked, taking out my notebook and pencil, which made Alpha laugh.

"Yes, seven years officially and we are working with the Asylum Seekers Council, in talks with the United Nations to see if we can have economic trade sanctions put in place for countries who are found to be allowing and profiting from FGM and the trafficking of these child brides overseas. I am in touch with the international trade centres across cities in Europe to help them identify the tell-tale signs of the sex trafficking routes and have them work with training the dock workers, again all whilst implementing heavy fines for those shipping companies who we know are involved. Of course, we are working with various police departments around the world on uncovering the vast networks of sex trafficking rings and doctors who work in gynaecology, mental health and reconstructive surgery. That's off the top of my head. Oh and the schools, colleges, Universities and BME Committees attached to various business organisations such as the Chambers of Commerce."

We walked in silence as we both took in the amount of action being taken by such a large group of people around the world and the gravitas of the organisations involved. "That's quite an impressive group of supporters, my lovely. You should be incredibly proud of yourself. Most people talk of taking action, but you have taken action. You do know what you have created here, don't you?" I asked.

"Well, I guess I do now. It has been a while since I have had to share what and who, and how long I have been working on this, and what I have, we have achieved together." Her voice trembled, taking it all in was obviously a lot for her. She looked out over the vast, open and beautiful hills of the Peak District, and with a smile on her face, I saw a tear roll down her right cheek.

"Are you okay, my lovely?" I asked her, placing my left arm around her waist.

She took a deep breath. "Yes, I am. Just taking it all in. The beauty here, and I don't just mean the beauty of this view, but the beauty of the people I have met, like Anwar and Jack who have introduced me to such influential people, who have networks and contacts they have reached out to and who have taken action and run with this movement. Men taking a stand for these women, when they are not of the same country, and not their women."

"Yeah, Jack and Anwar are very special men. And I

want to introduce you to Suleiman, although Anwar might have introduced you to him. He is running for president of Somalia, and he is a really lovely man, who has four daughters and has refused to allow them to be circumcised. He and his wife Fawzia are completely against this practice and was one of the reasons they came here to the UK. There are very few people who I would introduce you to on the larger political scale for this, other than a couple of my female friends who became Muslims. One of them is very high up in the legal system here in the UK and sits in the House of Lords, and another one who is a writer for a high profile political magazine. I am sure they would love to get involved with this project. You may know of them: Marina and Ayicha?"

Alpha looked at me. "No, I don't know these people but it would be an honour to be introduced to them to see how we can work together on this. Somalia has a terrible history of FGM and sex trafficking being hidden behind the blood diamonds. The distraction techniques at play in this world…"

Alpha trailed off, and I could see memories surfacing in her mind through her eyes and facial expressions.

"You know, I sometimes wonder how I got here, I wonder where I get my strength from, and some days I wonder why I bother. It is days like this, meeting women like you who believe in this movement and are willing to introduce me to such people that breaks and mends my heart all at the same time. I feel so sad for the girls in my nation who know no better, who deserve better, but they need educating. So do their parents and the wider community because it isn't just the FGM or the sex trafficking that is the problem, it is the demons in disguise who are so skilled at pretending and hiding who they are. The depths of betrayal in Africa need addressing. It is a HUGE project Moana and sometimes I feel like I am drowning in it all. Then I meet you and you give me air once more."

She sat down and took in a deep breath and then put her head in her hands. I stayed silent and looked out over the countryside spread out before me. It was stunning, and the boys and I had created many memories walking and climbing, and knew we would when we returned from Egypt, if we returned.

I heard her tears before I saw them, so sat on the rock beside hers. "I am not going to ask if you are okay, because it is obvious that you need to release whatever it is that has just come up for you. I am a good listener, and you know you need to tell me the backstory in one way or another, but if today is not that day, we can just walk and you can share whatever it is you need to share over time. No pressure."

She looked at me and although her eyes still danced with happiness, there was now a darkness in them that was hiding a deep pain and past fears overcome. "I want to share this; I have to share this. For you to truly understand the magnitude of what we are dealing with, and what we are up against. It isn't pleasant and my tears are for you as well as for me, because what I am about to share with you will stay with you always. Like those things you cannot unhear or unsee. Once you know this, you are going to imagine all kinds of horror, and you have to be ready to receive it. This isn't a movie, this isn't a crime novel, this is real life for millions of women around the world… and all for the pleasure and control of evil men, who raise their sons to be the same as them, and who raise their daughters to accept men like them. Africa is broken, and when Africa is broken, the world is broken. We are the heart of the world, the Queen of the world, why do you think the other nations stand either side of us and above us? To protect us. To allow our riches to shine outwards, but our men are evil and they dim our light under ego and corruption, power and greed. We need our brothers and sisters either side of Africa to work with us in bringing this evil to an end. This is why I stood and fought for my life, for my daughter's life, the lives of my sisters, all of them not just the sisters of blood, and this is why I stood alone for many years, outcast by my community, outcast by my family, and why the Angolan government wanted me dead, and would not stop until I was dead. England was the only safe refuge for me. And those of you who stand with me, you have to know the dangers. You have to know that by aligning yourself with my movement, it will not be safe for you to visit my country. So, I will tell you, but you must steel yourself Moana. And you must keep yourself and your children safe, at all costs. Do you hear me, my darling? Do you understand me?"

"Yes, I do. And yes I do. And yes I am ready to hear your story. And in time when my boys are older, they too will know your story. I stand with you, with all women fighting injustice, with all men who honour women, and themselves. Like you say, when Africa is broken the world is broken, but I say if one person's human rights are not recognised, then none of us have our human rights recognised. We are all connected and what happens may happen far away or out of sight and mind, but the ripple effect reaches far and wide, and we must join together and fight this. If I wouldn't want it done to me, then I must understand why I wouldn't, and then understand why it happens. Only from that place can I make the informed choices I need to make to know what to stand for, otherwise I stand for nothing."

"Jack and Anwar told me the night of our dinner you were the right woman Moana. They told me you were brave. That you would stand with me. Thank you my darling, from the depths of my heart and soul. Okay, I will tell you now. Let's walk some more sister." As she said this, I heard her Angolan accent come through stronger than ever. It was like she was being transported back to Angola, and her strength was coming through in her words, her voice as well as her focus on the trails ahead. She walked with a purpose, because she had a purpose, and that purpose was bigger than anything I had come across. I was unnerved, but I was ready.

If she could live through it and come out fighting, I could listen to it and fight with her.

FOUR
REFLECTIONS IN THE MUD

"I think, no I know, the defining moment for me was when I saw my little girl standing there looking down at me. Not my daughter, my husband had already sold her off to 'one of the greatest men in the congregation', a local businessman who was so wealthy, I couldn't even imagine the money he had. I am talking about the inner child that resides in all of us.

"To tell you about Mima, my daughter and only child first... I thought it very strange that a man such as this businessman would be interested in marrying into our family, and I knew, in every cell of my body that this match was not good and had evil behind it. The conversations with my daughter's future husband had been done without my involvement, which wasn't unheard of, but to be told that a match had been found and the wedding was taking place just two weeks later, my body reeled with pain, even more so when I saw the look of confusion on my daughter's face. She was barely twelve years old and had only just started her monthly bleeds. Life without my daughter would be cruel enough, but to know we only had two more weeks together broke me in ways I didn't know was humanly possible. She was my baby and still just a small child. This could not be happening. I begged and pleaded with my husband, but once again I felt the force of his punches rain down on me. Our daughter ran to her room and hid, I could hear her cries and I remember thinking, *At least she will be away from this. At least she will live a luxury life with this man as her husband.* I knew I was reassuring myself with lies. It is how we women get through the life we survive at the hands of a monster.

"My husband may have been the local pastor, a prestigious match for my parents' eldest daughter, but what people saw in church and in the street hid the calculated evil monster he was behind closed doors. When he proposed his hand in marriage to my parents, he had added a level of prestige to my family they had been seeking. My husband and his father, also a pastor, had been courting my family for a while, and although I told my parents repeatedly that I did not want to marry him, they forbid my fears being spoken. They told me the deal had already been done and I was not to bring shame on their family by refusing. As the date of my marriage to the pastor arrived, and the congregation celebrated, I hid in my misery, already afraid of this man who had threatened to make me sorry if I made him and his family fools on the very day he was to become my husband. The terror in his voice chilled me to the bone.

"He and my family were able to pass off my upset as a young woman leaving her family, and the nervous uncertainty of becoming a wife. I remember an Aunty looking at me with a gaze that told me she saw beyond the pretence of them all, and I felt as though she had reached a part of me that needed the love she sent my way. Our first night as husband and wife was incredibly painful. He forced himself upon me and within me. I cried out in pain and as he was inside of me, pushing his way in deeper and deeper. After he had finished and I saw the pool of blood I was laying in, I screamed out in fear. He punched me in the face to stop my screams and told me to get up and clean up my mess because 'seeing this mess was revolting'. This was how my marriage started and this is how it continued daily. He came and he took what he wanted, then he zipped up and walked away.

"My daughter was conceived during one of the nightly terrors of rape. In the beginning, I was too afraid to consider leaving, then I became numb to it all and just lay there whilst he did what he had to do. Like many women we were afraid of what was to come if we resisted, so we just let them use our bodies and took our minds elsewhere. I knew I was pregnant when I missed my monthly bleed, and I was both overjoyed with the thought of becoming a mother but terrified about what was to become of her life. I knew the past two years of not wanting to be married to him and my requests for help from my parents and Aunties fell on deaf ears.

"Knowing I was on my own and about to become a mother made something inside of me change. I didn't notice it at first, and even though I had learnt to play the dutiful pastor's wife, smiling and greeting all the dignitaries, dressing well and being seen in all the right places, I started to drop hints when in the company of certain ladies. I wanted to know if they too were living a life of terror. My conversations became bolder, using extracts of my story as someone else's story that I 'had heard about'. I watched the reactions of these women, I mentioned part of scripture where men were to honour the women, and how obeying didn't mean being a slave to the man. I watched the women and their interactions with their men, and I would invite some of the ladies to tea who had picked up on my messages with a deep look at me, a look one traumatised woman can spot in another woman.

"I knew these afternoon teas were a dangerous affair for both me and the women who attended, even though on the outside they appeared very innocent. My afternoon teas started to attract more and more women; the pastor became suspicious of these women arriving. He and his men had been talking about my soirees, had been discussing how dangerous it was for women to congregate in large numbers, and slowly but surely the beatings intensified, and not just for me, but for my women as well. Slowly but surely the women stopped coming and even though we had not addressed the violence in our homes, or our desire to leave the tyrants, we had come together because we knew the others knew what we were all going through.

"The longer sleeves meant bruises and lashing welts. The visiting of a friend meant the injuries were bad and needed hiding away from public eyes. The limp as we walked meant the rape and the beatings had been particularly violent, and the young girls disappearing was more than them being eaten by the lions and the panthers or taken by the rebels, as was reasoned by the men. These young girls were being sold by their fathers, after their monthly bleeds had started, to the highest bidder, all orchestrated by my husband the pastor as he was the one who blessed each girls cutting, 'her arrival into womanhood' even at the tender ages of five and six. These girls were not entering womanhood, they were being groomed by the men who they called Pai. The men they trusted to protect them. This is why the birth of a girl had become even more celebrated than the birth of a son.

"Our sons were being sold into slavery in the mines, to produce wealth for the Americans, the Dutch in South Africa and the Russians. Diamonds may be a girl's best friend in the white west, but to us African ladies they were the stuff of nightmares. Our voices silenced because the world was more worried about the war, which was funded by these precious gems. The term 'conflict diamonds' preferred over 'blood diamonds' because to call them 'blood diamonds' would bring home that blood one had spilled on the diamonds around their necks and wrists or hanging from their ears. To know that another woman's son had been killed so the women in the west could sparkle at the ball was too much for the high society. If they knew that the civil war was hiding the terror we women faced in our own homes, that our vaginas were mutilated at a young age by men who did not have any medical training whatsoever, and then our daughters were being sold as sex slaves to our leaders and businessmen, would they have done anything? Could they have done anything? Or were these women more terrified by our truth, because that would highlight the truth of the men they were married to?

"When my daughter was born I secretly wished for her

to be plain in her features, to not be beautiful, because to be beautiful would mean a certainty of marriage at a young age. Looking at my husband and my own features, when they were not swollen, cut or bruised, I knew my daughter would be a beautiful young thing. It would be her curse, and mine.

"When she was born, the whole town celebrated, none more so than my husband and his friends. Some of my ladies looked at me with pity, because they knew these men were not cheering the birth of a beautiful baby girl for the reasons they should be as a proud and happy father, that his wife had given him a daughter to protect, teach and enjoy conversations of the heart and mind, but because he knew in twelve years' time he would be so much richer due to the dowry which would be paid for her.

"The day he sold her I remember screaming at him and beating him, only to receive the beating of my life which left me face down in the mud at the back of our home. It was February, and we were in the middle of the rainy season. The pastor had dragged me out of our home by my hair and beaten me so badly I could not move to defend myself. He continued to beat me with the stick he used to wave at the wild animals and left me for dead. I don't know how long I was there for, hours maybe, but when I came round, it wasn't just dark of night, with the moon shining down, it was the darkest day of my life so far. My precious baby girl was gone, and I knew in my bones I would never see her again.

"As I tried to pick myself up my body raged with pain and my arms gave way. My right arm was broken, so I pushed myself up with my left, and that is when I saw my reflection in the muddy water. The moon is a beautiful thing, but that night I didn't know whether to curse the moon for it's bright light or thank it, for it was this event in my life which gave me the power I needed to start the movement. I knew angels were looking down on me. I didn't know it would be a movement, I just knew I could not stay with this monster any more.

"I dragged myself back into the house, and did my best to clean myself up, because if he came to me and wanted to use my body for gratification again, and I was in the muddy and bloody mess I was in, he would beat me again. It didn't matter to him that my body and my face were broken or bruised, it actually excited him more as it reminded him of his power over me. He did not come to me that night, and I fell asleep in fear and exhaustion waiting for him.

"When I woke up the next morning, I could only just see the true extent of my injuries through the swelling of my eyes. I had patches of hair missing, my lips were so swollen I could hardly move them and my nose was broken. I wrapped my right arm in tight bandages with a wooden spoon along my forearm as a splint and used one of my many scarves to make a sling. I could not tie my hair in my usual style of scarf so I improvised with one of the many wigs I had for our prestigious social gatherings.

"I shuffled into the kitchen and noticed the day was the 22nd of February, and I nodded to the calendar. This day would be my new beginning, because I knew if I could pick myself up with dignity from the ordeal of the day before, I could do anything. This was no longer about me, this was about my daughter, and all the other daughters of Africa who were being raped, beaten and mutilated."

Alpha stood up, turned to me and then looked out at the countryside in front of us. "You know in some ways this reminds me of my town Caxito back home in Angola. When you get away from the main road it is beautiful and you would never believe the atrocities that we experienced. Being so close to Luanda, the capitol of Angola, we have the main train tracks and major roads in and out of the city which made the trafficking easier. With the major ports being in Luanda to the rest of the world in the west via the Atlantic, our girls could disappear without a trace really quickly. It also meant that the diamonds which were being used to fund the war, were also used in paying off the merchants in the shipping companies. Everyone profited from the diamonds and the girls of Angola, except the women. When I come up here to be by myself, I feel like I am home. I feel at peace."

The sadness in her voice was so different to the woman who had been singing away in her car just a couple of hours before, and yet the strength she exuded was stronger than it had been at the event and our dinner with Jack and Anwar. It was almost as if reliving the experience by telling me had given her an extra dose of fortitude. She stood taller, and there was an air of defiance about her that spoke volumes.

"Did you want to walk a bit further out? Or shall we turn back and head into Hathersage for a coffee and a bit of lunch?" I asked her.

"You know, I am a tad hungry and I could do with a fresh pot of coffee if truth be told. So yes, let's turn back and go get some lunch… and cake. I am in the mood for some cake. How does the best café and Victoria Sponge cake grab you?"

"You had me at cake, and to know it is Victoria Sponge cake won me over completely!" I replied. We linked arms again and the cheery Alpha was back.

"You know I see her face everywhere. Sometimes I see a little girl and think it is her, but I know she will be twenty by now, if she was alive," she said.

"What do you mean, if she was alive? Do you not believe she is?" I asked.

"No, sadly I don't. It was about a year, eighteen months after she had been sold to that man, and I felt this shudder run through me as if part of me had died. Up until then I had held out hope that one day she may escape him, but that day, I felt such an intense sadness and grief, and I just knew. I think every mother knows when her child dies. We know when a loved one dies if we have a strong connection with them, and there is no stronger connection to someone else than that of a birth mother and their beloved child," she replied with such a melancholy feel to her.

"I'm sorry to hear this, but in some ways I am not. Living with a man who could buy you, and do all those terrible things to you – at any age, not just at the age of twelve – which we are both assuming as we have no proof, must have been horrendous, so I hope she did escape, either by running away or by passing away."

Alpha stood and looked at me. I felt as though I had upset her with my comment about not having the proof of what this man had done to her daughter, but instead I saw a smile breaking through. "You know, no one has ever had the courage to say that to me before, even if they have been thinking it. And you are right, we do not have any proof of what this man did or didn't do to my daughter. All I know is, if he had dealings with the pastor, then he was no good. Either that or it was an undercover police officer gathering evidence. If it was the second option though, why did no one come for me? Surely she would have told them what we both experienced at the pastors hands and the police would have known I was not behind it?

"I have wondered so many times if I was right to judge this man so harshly, but again, if he was a good man and he had no ill intentions, why did he not make contact with me, Mimi's mother and help me escape too? The honest and only explanations are: that he was as evil as the pastor; he died trying to help these young girls and so could not get in touch with me; or he thought I was involved in the sale of my daughter and left me to rot alongside the pastor.

"I know there are many men who are complicit without actually knowing they are. They are 'just the driver' escorting the young girls to see their aunties and uncles, or to a new school, or being sent home to their loving parents, who are no more than the traffickers. I also know that there are men accused of all sorts of evil and they are completely innocent in all of this. I have met doctors who have practiced FGM for many years, and when they discover the true depths of the problems they cause for these women, and wake up out of the cultural slumber, they join us in the fight against it. These are some of our best spokespeople as they have woken up and start working against their culture, their families and travel to other African countries to raise awareness. Men are our biggest allies in this fight to stop FGM, and I honour the ones who stand tall and fight beside us.

"For you to say what you did to my face, a grieving mother, takes courage. Thank you."

"I don't really see it as courage, but I will take that compliment from you. I see it as really needing facts before accusing others and making sure that when we are sharing this information with the people I need to share this with, I have all the accurate facts, because once these people know, and the investigations we do start to uncover facts, we need to make sure there are no doubts in our minds about who is and who is not involved. And I know you appreciate that, and respect that."

We got back to the car park and Alpha stopped. By her feet was a puddle. She looked down at it and nodded. Then looked up at me and saw I had seen her gesture. She winked at me, unlocked her car and we got in. "Right then, coffee and cake. Let's go!"

FIVE

SILENCE PROMOTES VIOLENCE

Sitting in the café looking at the menu we were both distracted.

Me by what I had just been told, and Alpha because, "I don't even know which part of the story to tell you next. You know the horrifying life I lived with the pastor, and about the movement, and I wonder what you would like to know next. Not that you would 'like' to know next, because it certainly isn't something to like. That said, I am going to have the quiche, jacket potato and side salad. What are you having?" she asked.

"I was thinking the exact same thing! About all of it, not just the food," I replied giving her a cheeky grin. "I would like to know more about the ladies at your soirees and what happened to them, if you know."

"I do know, and I think that is a good place to continue. You see these ladies were married to powerful men, ones who were used to getting their own way. These ladies had lives of luxury, and although some of them had beatings, not all of them were as severe as mine, and mine were not as severe as others. In comparison what I went through was a tiny slap. Some of these women were paralysed with fear, and so them simply being in attendance at my soirees was a very brave thing to do.

"I started them again you know, well I didn't start them, I just continued inviting the ladies to join me. Some days there would be three or four of us, and other days there would be around twenty of us. All dancing around the subject of why we were there and speaking in some kind of code that we all understood without explanation.

"We knew that the longer we remained silent, the more the violence would continue, and not just for us, but for our daughters. The women who had sons also didn't want them to be like their fathers. Some talked hypothetically about 'these women who escape', some talked about 'getting away with murder', some used the phrases of 'starting over' whilst others just remained silent and took in all that was being said. There were a few women who never said a word and at times I would wonder if they were spying on us for the men, but one day one of these silent ladies spoke up and silenced us all: 'Whilst we speak in codes, and some of us remain silent, we are still not taking action. We can talk all we want but the truth is we are married to rapists, paedophiles and men who trade in sex slaves. Slavery was abolished, even in South Africa slavery was abolished, and yet here it is in our very own homes, and we are allowing it to happen. We cannot allow this to carry on any more, we just cannot. I am sick and tired, in the literal and the physical sense ladies. Of hearing us excuse these men, of dressing up in our finery and pretending we are in love with these monsters to further their businesses so they can make more profit and buy more little girls, all at the permission and facilitation of the pastor and Doctor Bayen'.

"We ladies looked at each other, and I and Doctor Bayen's wife dropped our heads in shame as the other ladies knew it was our husbands who were indeed the ones facilitating this. We both knew we, more than the other ladies, had a bigger duty to these ladies than the rest of them."

"Why did you think that?" I asked.

Alpha waited a moment as our orders were taken and the coffees we had ordered on the way in were delivered to our table.

"Why did we think we had a bigger duty than the rest of the ladies? Because they were our husbands, and yes we were victims of their crimes also, but they were our husbands, and knowing it is your husband who is arranging the cutting and the sale of these young girls was a heavy burden.

"One of the other ladies spoke up and defended us by stating: 'We cannot point the blame solely at the feet of the pastor and the doctor. All our men are responsible, we are equally responsible for all the deaths of these little girls on the cutting table and in the events that follow. I agree that we must do something, but how can we overturn the tradition of our people which dates back over 2000 years. Female circumcision is as old as our ancestors who walked this land, and the sex slavery is as old as the Portuguese rule of our lands. What we are about to do is change the course of history of our country, and for Africans as a whole. We must ask ourselves if we are ready for this, and if we are going to stand firm and strong together'.

"Then a woman who had been coming to my soirees on and off, more nervous each time whispered: 'I do not know how I can help you ladies as you are so brave even saying the things you are saying. I am already scared just being here in the room with you'.

"I wondered if it was her beatings, and when I heard her voice, the fear within it, and the power of these other ladies, I knew we had a core number to start something. I also realised that it would take a huge amount of courage for the rest of my ladies to stand up and be counted." Alpha stopped what she was sharing as our lunch arrived.

"I like how you call them your ladies," I said. "Why do you call them this?"

"Because they are my ladies, we are all ladies together. You are one of my ladies. This is an African thing. We do not say friends, nor girlfriends. We are women, we are ladies and when we stand together we become ladies of the highest calibre," replied Alpha with a big cheesy grin on her face. I wasn't sure if it was due to the smell of the quiche and the fact the jacket potato was actually a jacket potato with a proper oven baked crispy jacket rather than the microwaved imposter that had become the norm, or whether it was because she had just realised I was one of her ladies, either way it was good to see that big smile on her face after a morning of her reliving some awful memories.

"So I am one of your ladies, am I?" I asked teasing her, knowing full well I was one of her ladies, regardless of how little time we had known each other.

"Well, if you haven't demanded I take you home already after what you have heard this morning, and you are still wanting to know more about the backstory, then yes, you are. Jack and Anwar both said we would become good friends, and after everything they have helped me with, I trust them, and you can imagine how hard it was for me to trust a man after everything I had been through and witnessed."

"Did they now? Well... other than them arranging my friendship circles," I said smiling, "and between the projects we have worked on together, they are really great guys. They are genuine and I love how they call the bullshit out of the disingenuous shallow business owners in the city. We have seen some real prestige hunters over the years, people wanting to say they belong to a project, or a board committee and they never show up or walk their grandiose talk they love spouting. I am sure they would never had recommended me to you for a project like this or set us up at that lecture if they thought we would not work well together."

"You think they set us up to meet?" asked Alpha.

"Yes, I do. Tell me, how did you know about the event we met at? And when did you find out about it?" I asked her.

"Well, Jack told me about it when it was in the planning stages and told me I had to be there," she responded.

"Okay, and did he say anything else about the event?"

"Well, he told me that there would be people at the event I would want to meet, and needed to meet."

"Okay, well, about two weeks before the event, I got an

email from Jack telling me about the event and he told me that I would want to be part of it before I headed off to Egypt, and that there would be people I would want to meet and needed to meet. Sound familiar?" I said smiling.

"Cheeky bugger!" laughed Alpha. "Almost word for word except the part about Egypt."

"Yep… and you know what?"

"What?" she asked.

"You really have been in Yorkshire for a while, the phrases you come out with, the' be proper Yorkshur luv'. You'll be saying 'tinterweb' next." We both laughed really loudly, much to the annoyance of a couple of old ladies sat near to us.

"We're being frowned upon you know," she whispered to me.

"Ah, who cares. People will always frown upon those who are enjoying themselves, or sat looking miserable, or better dressed, worse dressed, or something. Let them stare and frown, and let's wait a few more minutes before we order that delicious looking cake over there."

The waitress came over and took our plates, and we praised the jacket potatoes for being proper jacket potatoes, and we all laughed loudly together. "We pride ourselves on being the only café in the area who doesn't have a microwave."

Alpha and I both agreed that microwaves were toxic and should be banned and the waitress gave us a few more minutes to digest the food whilst we continued our conversation.

"So what happened after your shy lady spoke up?" I asked Alpha, wanting to continue the conversation.

"We assured her that we were all scared just being together in the room. A few of the ladies shared the beatings they had received from their husbands after they had found out about them attending our 'afternoon teas' which is what I had called them. Tears fell, and the energy in the room changed. It was the first time any of us had openly admitted we were beaten, and how bad they were. With each story we became stronger, not just in ourselves, but together. We were now united in knowledge, and slowly but surely every woman in the room had shared her story, even the shy woman. We knew we had to do something because it wasn't just us that experienced our beatings, it was our daughters and our sons and we knew that when we stayed silent and just accepted the beatings we were teaching our children we were worthless and deserved these beatings, that they were to be and expect the same in their future.

"Hands were held, and reassurance given to one another. We all agreed we would do something to stop these beatings, and we would start sharing that it was our bodies and we were not going to allow ourselves to be raped any more. Ideas were shared about creating leaflets, putting graffiti on walls in town, and having conversations with the ladies in our towns and villages secretly.

"Some of them became emboldened, and others I could see were scared, but we all agreed we had to do something. Our vaginas had been mutilated when we were younger, so sex was painful enough for all of us, without men forcing themselves on us and making it even more painful. Some of the ladies shared they were scared to get pregnant again because the birth had been excruciating and they were cut all over again. The husbands didn't care and took to having sex with them the same night and with even more force and enthusiasm because he had been out celebrating becoming a father again. It was a vicious cycle that just kept continuing. Vagina gets cut, man rapes woman, woman gets pregnant and then cut again, man rapes woman. And on and on it goes.

"Sharing our stories made us all realise what monsters we lived with and that we were not alone. A woman, who had been one of the quieter ladies, then asked a few questions which used to haunt me until I came here. She asked, 'How many of us have been outside of our country? Or even our towns and cities? How many of us know that marriage is any different to what we are experiencing?'

"When the rest of us ladies heard these questions, even though we didn't have the answer to if marriage was any different in other countries, we knew what we were experiencing wasn't right. Until one woman spoke up: 'We know in our bones it is not right. We know from the scriptures this isn't right. We know from raising our sons that they are kind and gentle, until we allow their fathers to take control of them. We know, we have seen it with other women that they are not afraid of their husbands. We are all very good at faking our pleasure of serving our husbands in public, but we all recognised within each other that we experience something other women do not. Marriage is not supposed to be like this and I refuse to believe every man is a monster. My father wasn't a monster. Your father was not a monster. You know this evil is a curse from the civil war and has been brought into our homes because of the violence it has unleashed in our men. We are not born evil, we are born good and our men have become conditioned by the evil and the greed of the white man, and we will only be free of this tyranny in our country and in our homes when we become more like the white woman who we have been led to believe is unruly and disrespectful. She is only unruly because she does not allow the man to rule her. She is only disrespectful of those who show her disrespect and until we negro women learn how to respect ourselves more and rule ourselves, then we will never be free of these evil monsters who share our homes and our beds'.

"I remember the surprise on the faces of my ladies, and then the cheer that went up from us all. We felt empowered for the first time in a long time – well, for the first time. This lady, her name was Hadiza had been one of the quieter in our group. She was one of the most respected women in the town due to the way in which she worked really hard on her land. You have to remember Moana, that it is the women who work the land and produce the food in our country, and even after we have been beaten we still tend to the land and go to the market to sell our fruits and vegetables. It is us that prepare the meat which our men have gone to the plains to hunt. As women of standing in our community based on who our husbands were, we did not do as much as the women who tended the land, but we still had to get up and see to the growing and tending of our farms. Hadiza showed us that we had been blind to the poorer men, who were kind and gentle with their families. The men who played with their children. She reminded us that we were only seeing evil in men because we experienced so much of it, but when we opened our eyes to the other men in our communities we would see that the men surrounding us were good and kind.

"One of the things which would stop us from producing leaflets would be that many of us were illiterate, like the majority of the women in Africa. We would need an ally, one who was able to read and write, and help us produce these leaflets we wanted to share in the food packages women would collect from one another in the markets.

"This meeting was one of the most exciting meetings I have ever had because it was the start of something great, something greater than us, something for our daughters, for our sons, for our country, and for women the world over. I just never realised until I came here to the UK, just how widely spread these problems are. Learning about the rape within marriage happening to so many women of all walks of life, and how women are blamed for it, not just by the men themselves but by other women. Learning how it didn't matter if you were rich or poor, educated or not, black, white or Asian, rape within marriage is one of the most unspoken truths we women experienced.

"To learn that FGM happens in almost every country in the world, and to then understand that many of the women who died back home in Angola had not died of natural causes, but from the after effects of the cutting, such as cysts; death due to haemorrhaging in childbirth because of the way her vagina had been cut; all of these things I have learnt and shared with the ladies back home has helped them, helped other women. But sometimes it feels as though this is a never ending problem. Some days, like this day when we all shared our stories for the first time, we feel as though we have conquered a mountain, but other days all we see are many more mountains, it is hard to continue. And then we meet people like Jack, Anwar, Dr Costa, and you."

We sat in silence for a moment, with our thoughts and Alpha raised her hand for the waitress to bring our cake and a fresh pot of tea over to us.

"I think this is a perfect time for cake, don't you?"

"I do believe you are right, and then we can walk. Move this information and energy through our systems. What says you?"

"I do believe you are right, a walk in the fresh air always does us good," Alpha replied, placing her hand on mine. "Thank you, Moana. Thank you for listening, for being here, and for agreeing to join us."

I didn't remember saying I would join her in her movement, but after hearing what I had just heard, what kind of woman would I be if I didn't join these women, even if it was by raising awareness in my own way? Ignoring it would only allow it to continue and knowing about it and doing nothing about it made me as guilty as those who wielded the scalpel that cuts the vaginas of these women. I had to get involved, there was nothing else I could do.

SIX
CUTS OF PURITY

Returning home that night, I wanted to know more and more about the process of cutting both the female genitalia as well as diamonds. To me it made sense. If the diamonds were supposedly funding the civil war and stopping the plight of these women from being heard, then both needed looking into.

The world was outraged by the likes of Tiffany, Cartier and Harry Winston possibly being connected to 'blood diamonds', and god forbid a Harry Winston didn't have a pure cut diamond which reflected colour and clarity, so why were they not outraged by the cutting of baby girls who were days old and up to the age of puberty?

Both were cut to demand a high price, and to supposedly signify purity, so in my mind the two were essential reading.

I soon realised that red and brown diamonds were the conflict diamonds, even though the red diamond was considered the most expensive per carat. I wondered why this was and wanted to know if they were one and the same? I discovered that in the process of becoming a red diamond, the diamond itself was formed differently, much like the healing process following the cutting of the clitoris and labias, and although the formation of red diamonds had nothing to do with man, the formation process of these young girls vaginas had everything to do with the butchering they received at the hand of men.

Was the cutting only performed by men was my next question? I was shocked to find out that the circumcision was normally carried out by older women and could not believe that another woman could cause such harm to another woman's genitalia. Was this because the woman wanted to protect the young girls from improper behaviour by man? Or was it because they wanted to make sure it was done in the least harmful way possible? Or had women become so brainwashed that they really did not see this as a harmful thing to do, especially given that it was done to curb women's pleasure and sexual promiscuity! Why on earth would another woman want to stop a woman from enjoying sex, and cause so many health problems? I kept thinking of Munchausen's Syndrome and then Stockholm Syndrome, neither of which fitted but characteristics of both still stuck in my mind.

Keeping a woman chaste had been the operandi in so many cultures for centuries and the more I read the more I reflected on my own sexuality. Had I been psychologically chaste in some way due to being 'Oh so terribly British' and protecting myself by dressing modestly to prevent male attention? Had the very idea of monogamy been a way of keeping people chaste because over the years, apparently in marriage the sex drive is lost and sex wasn't a thing. What about masturbation? We had been told from a very young age that if we masturbated we would turn blind, and then I remembered a girl from college who was caught masturbating having really thick glasses, and even though I was old enough to know that an old wives tale was just that, there is always an underlying truth in them somewhere. Just how far had we fallen when we could not enjoy our own bodies and had other people mutilate our minds and our bodies so we did not enjoy sex.

Then my mind wandered even further. Was the fact that women had twice as many nerve endings in their clitoris than men had in the end of their penis the reason these men, and women, wanted to cut away the very thing that gave us this pleasure? Highly doubtful as most people were unaware of this basic fact of the human anatomy.

I then considered that it was necessary for all women to learn how to pleasure their man and turn him into the multi-orgasmic man, as I had been learning how to do. Instead of reducing the woman's sexual desires, why not increase both the man and woman's sexual desire? Raise each other up rather than dumb each other down as we were seeing the world over in various aspects of life, such as people being easily offended by something they disagreed with and strong people having to be gentle with those who refused to strengthen themselves.

As I continued reading I wanted to know why some people prefer to call this awful procedure female circumcision rather than genital mutilation? Was this to normalise the procedure, to ease their consciences? Or was it because they didn't understand the real trauma these women go through once they have been mutilated?

Learning about the different kinds of circumcision made some kind of sense, depending on which category it fell into. I couldn't believe what I was reading! There were four categories recognised by medical practitioners! And doctors in the west were performing the very act of cutting away a woman's pleasure centre.

The more I read, the more questions I had, the more questions I had, the more I read, the angrier I got. How could they do this to a woman! I looked into the reasons it was done, and it all came down to either tradition, which had its origins in controlling sexual promiscuity. Then there were documents online which said that it was an Islaamic procedure and I knew that was a crock of shit, and not just because Alpha was Christian but because many of the African countries it was taking place in were not Islaamic, they were Christian. I knew this was a media hate campaign to make even more people turn against Muslims and give organisations such as Britain First and the English Defence League (EDL) more fuel for their already existing hatred of the 'brown faces' and 'rag heads' as they referred to the Muslims and immigrants that had come to England to escape civil war in their own countries, predominantly started by British interference with their trusted allies across the pond – the good old U S of A.

I messaged Alpha. *We need to talk. I have been researching all the questions I had but didn't have time to ask you today and been looking at the procedures and the biology of the clitoris. Women actually do this to each other????*

I hit send, and almost as soon as I had sent it, I had a response. *Was just going to ask you how the research was going, and I am sure you have had a visual feast this evening.*

Before I could reply, her next message came. *Yes, women do this to each other, that is why we have the education sector of the movement to educate the women and young girls so it becomes a dying 'art' – Would you and the boys like to come over for dinner tomorrow evening?*

I responded. *That would be lovely, but I am not sure I want to discuss this with the boys around.*

Her response to that made me stop in my tracks. *And why would that be? Are they not capable of understanding? And why hide it from them? They have been circumcised and you want to raise awareness don't you?*

She had me. I had no answer other than, *What time is dinner? And would you like us to bring a dish of our own?*

If we were going to start changing things in Africa, Asia and in the countries where this barbaric practice took place, including here in the UK, and overseas in Europe and America then we needed everyone in our society to know. We had to normalise talking about it with our children. My boys were old enough to know about bits of it and have it explained to them in simplistic terms, and with our up and coming move to Egypt, it would be even more important for them to know about it at some point so why not from their own mother and an incredible woman who had been through the traumas she had been through and had a very positive outcome of transforming the lives of these other women?

I went back to my research, learning about the conditions this was done under made very uncomfortable reading. There were many times I tightened my pelvic floor muscles in solidarity and discomfort.

The biggest consensus was that it was a way of not

only curbing sexual promiscuity but also to avoid social exclusion. It was a distorted sense of protecting the girls from being rejected by other women and when they came of age, a way of stopping them from enjoying sex so much that they looked for it elsewhere. I couldn't understand this because if a husband delighted his wife sexually then why would she need to go elsewhere?

Asking myself this question once again made me look at my own marriage. Was I giving my husband enough pleasure to stop him going elsewhere? Was he giving me enough pleasure to stop me going elsewhere? Well, the thought of cheating on my husband hadn't even crossed my mind. I was more than happy with my husband on every level, and I would have been more than willing to experiment in any and all areas of sex. I was intrigued by bondage, and dominatrix but not the sadomasochist area. That was a bit too much for me. There's the pleasure-pain heights of sexual pleasure and there is playful bondage and dominance, but anything that goes beyond that I was not interested in.

I continued researching for a few more hours and didn't finish until 1 am. This was such a complex subject and didn't have an easy solution. Alpha was right though, this needed a multifaceted approach through educational awareness, political sanctions and medical practices; when I woke up the following morning, I would get cracking on a list of ideas, contacts and organisations who I thought would be able to help in one way or another.

Waking up the next morning, the clarity I had on the various names and organisations flowed through me like water into the ocean from a raging river. I leapt up out of bed, and put the kettle on, went to the loo and started putting up the A1 sheets of flip chart paper. I placed three up on the wall and wrote the words: Education – Political – Medical in the middle of each one. One word to a sheet. I then drew the CND symbol over the top of the word so each page was divided into three aspects and then I grabbed my marker pens. I didn't even check the time, and it wasn't until the alarm went off to wake the boys up I realised that I hadn't even given them a second thought, and when I looked at the sheets of paper, they were almost full. I would need more paper.

I went through to the boys room and woke them up ready for school and nursery, and then went back through to the kitchen to finish off making the coffee I had boiled the kettle for over an hour before.

I loved mornings like this and I don't think I had been this fired up for a very long time. Whilst I was making the boys breakfast, and they were getting dressed, more and more ideas were swirling around in my mind. The boys came running down the stairs shouting, "Breakfast! Yeah! Morning Mummy! How are you? Did you sleep well?"

"Yes my angels, did you?"

"Yeah I did!" replied Marai.

"And I did!" shouted Salah.

"Well I can't answer for you, can I?" tutted Marai, rolling his eyes.

They sat at the table and then looked at what I had been doing all morning. "What's that for? And what does FGM mean Mummy?" asked Marai.

"Well, it means that when little girls are born or a little

bit older, around your age, some people believe that they should have their private parts cut away," I replied.

"Owwwwchh!!! That's not nice!" declared Marai holding his private parts.

Salah laughed, "Marai is holding his peanuts!!"

"Salah this is not funny, these little girls are having their peanuts cut off!" replied Marai.

"Whaaatt??? Why?? Who would do that? That's just wrong," declared Salah, before adding, "Mummy can I have some more cereal please?"

"Yes baby, you can, and it is wrong," I replied.

"So why do that do it Mummy?" asked Marai.

"Because some people think it makes women easier to control when they get older," I answered.

"But how do they pee if they don't have their willy and peanuts?" Salah asked me.

"Girls don't have peanuts and a willy silly," said Marai.

"Willy Silly," laughed Salah, "and if they don't have peanuts and a willy… how do people cut it off?"

I could see this was going to become an interesting conversation and it wasn't one I was expecting to have so early in the boys' lives, but now was as good a time as any, and their innocence around the whole thing was making it easy to formulate my own thoughts around this. I also knew that I would more than likely get a call from the school and nursery due to conversations the boys were probably going to have, especially Salah. No doubt he would be telling the girls at nursery to mind out for their peanuts being cut off, so I prepared myself for those conversations, but they never came.

I knew this breakfast story would bring a smile to

Alpha's face when we saw her for dinner later that night, and when the boys asked me what was for dinner when they got home, I told them, "We are going to see one of mummy's new friends for dinner."

"Did she have her peanuts cut off?" asked Salah

I hesitated for a moment before responding with, "Well, why don't you ask her when we see her later."

"That means she has then," said Marai.

"Eeewww!!" said Salah grabbing his own peanuts.

"Salah!" Marai scolded him.

"What Marai? It hurts just thinking about it! Don't your peanuts hurt when you think about it?

"Well yeah, it makes them feel smaller," Marai replied.

I couldn't help but smile away to myself listening to my three year-old and seven year-old discussing FGM in the most innocent of ways and understanding how it hurt their 'peanuts' just thinking about it. Progress was already being made… one young mind at a time.

SEVEN

RISKING IT ALL FOR PEANUTS

Arriving at Alpha's home that night for dinner, the first words out of Salah's mouth was, "Aunty Alpha, Mummy told us to ask you if you had your peanuts removed, so have you?"

Marai reminded him that girls didn't have peanuts, and I wanted the ground to swallow me up.

Alpha on the other hand roared with laughter. "Peanuts you call them hey? Well… yes I have, and I am doing my best to help stop other ladies having their peanuts removed too."

"Good. Because it hurts me thinking about it. I have to cross my legs as if I needed a wee. May I have a drink please, Aunty?"

Alpha looked at me as she giggled away to herself and ruffled Salah's hair. "Well, you're quite the character, aren't you!"

"I can be any character I want to be, Iron Man, the Red Power Ranger, Robin Hood… I have all the outfits at home. I didn't bring them with me though. We did bring books with us though and Marai has homework to do. Do you need any help with dinner, Aunty?"

Alpha looked at Salah and they continued their conversation about characters they liked to play whilst I sat and helped Marai with his homework. Over dinner the boys had so many questions about Angola, and how Alpha came to England and when they asked how she was going to help save the peanuts of all the girls in Angola and the world, she told the boys I was going to help her and her team around the world.

"Are we going to help save the girls in Egypt when we get there, Mummy?" asked Marai.

"I don't know yet Baaba. I have to do a lot of research when we get there, and then we will see," I replied.

"I think you should Mummy, because if the girls don't have peanuts then how can they have babies properly? You nearly died having Salah, and that was scary, and you have your peanuts, don't you?"

"Yes Baaba, I do have my peanuts, and yes it was really scary," I told him.

"You know Marai, I was able to have a daughter without my peanuts, and it was very painful, and yes many women die when they have a baby. Some ladies can't have children because it hurts them to even get pregnant, or when the man or woman removes their peanuts it can cause them many problems so they can't get pregnant," added Alpha.

The boys sat there and thought about what Alpha had said and then Salah said, "Well, I think it is horrible and I think you should stop people cutting the peanuts off girls. Do they do it to boys too, because if they do, I don't want to go to Angolia."

"It's Angola, Salah," corrected his brother, before looking at Alpha and asking her, "How many people are helping you, Aunty? Are there lots of people, because Mummy wrote down lots of names on her papers on the wall this morning, and Mummy knows lots of people who will help you, don't you Mummy?"

All three of them turned to me looking expectant. "I do know a few people Baaba, and yes I will be helping Aunty Alpha with her project," I said looking at Alpha, this being the first time I had confirmed out loud that I would be helping.

"Good, I am glad you are going to help Mummy. Please may we get down from the table now please?" asked Marai.

"Yes Baaba, you can. Just take your plates through to the kitchen and then finish your homework."

"Thank you, and I've already finished it. Come on Salah let's go and read our books," Marai said as he took Alpha's plate and mine with his own to the kitchen."

The boys occupied themselves with their books while Alpha and I continued to sit at the table and discuss what had happened back in Angola after the meeting when all the ladies came together and shared their stories.

"After that first meeting we met a few more times and ideas were flowing on how we were going to spread the word, and how we were going to reach the people who needed to be reached. As you know many women perform the cutting, especially the older ladies, so it was necessary we spoke with them and got them to stop. We knew it wasn't going to be a one conversation process, and it was going to be more and more about asking questions as to why us women were experiencing the different things we were experiencing. Some of us were unable to get pregnant, others bled very heavily and some of us were in chronic pain with hard lumps protruding from our tummies. These elderly ladies either knew deep down these were all results of the cutting and the older we were the more the symptoms showed, or they had not been able to connect the dots and just put it down to being a woman. It was a matter of helping them connect the dots to the cutting they were performing on us all and finding the information to present to them.

"You have to remember that we don't have computers or the internet readily available in Angola like we do here in the UK so getting hold of this information was a dangerous thing to do. Some of the ladies who could read would go into Luanne on the bus and visit the libraries looking for books on anatomy. Doctor Bayen's wife looked in his medical journals and bit by bit we were able to gather drawings and bits of information to put in our own leaflets. We started having our afternoon teas in different places so more ladies could come along and slowly but surely we began to realise these ladies were beginning to grow in confidence. One lady suggested that we took to the streets at the next political gathering. Many didn't feel ready for that and so we agreed that until the numbers of ladies who did feel ready grew, we would just keep meeting and having our 'afternoon teas'. They were working, and then one night we heard that one of our ladies had been raped to death by her husband. This was all the courage we needed."

"Raped to death?" I confirmed shocked by what I had heard.

"Yes, he had been smoking Ibogaine, a hallucinogenic plant found in Angola, Cameroon and a few other countries. He was coming out the other side of the trip when he arrived home and just kept raping her and raping her until he split her and she bled out. We found out that he had also suffocated her, no doubt because she had tried to scream out in pain. It was Doctor Bayen who was called to her house and his wife had accompanied him which was pretty normal practice late at night. She described the scene to us without much detail but the detail she shared with us was horrendous. We knew we had to add marital rape into our campaign, rather than just focusing on FGM.

"This could have been any of us, because Ibogaine was common. We were safe at the beginning of the trip because the men were rendered useless because it affects the muscles first and then the trip starts. Many men have used it in very small doses to help with the hunting as it really heightens their senses and sitting in the same position for long periods of time they get cramp. The thing is, like with any drug the more you do it, the more tolerance you have to it, and some men get arrogant and forget they are dealing with Mother Nature. She doesn't measure accurately how much of a dose she puts into each leaf, root or flower and so sometimes the doses the men take can send them into delirium for days.

"The determination with which my ladies came

together after that was stronger than the first day when we shared our stories, and it was this day that we decided to take to the streets. We spread the word which was difficult because we had to keep this a secret from the men. Our problem was going to be getting from our town to Luanne, as this was going to be the best place to demonstrate. We agreed on a date to travel by bus and some by train, meeting by the main parliament building, as there were already protests there about the 200 million US Dollars the conflict diamonds had raised to build the new parliament building. It was denied by everyone that this is where the money came from, but we Angolans may be poor but we are not stupid. Our country is funded by diamonds and oil, and terror. Terror in our homes, in the streets, in the mines, and in the parliament.

We knew that by us all heading to Luanda we would have a better chance of being heard by international news stations, and we were right. Those of us who turned up…" she trailed off.

"What do you mean 'those of us who turned up'?" I asked her.

"Well, many of the women chose not to travel on the day, too afraid of what would be waiting for them when they returned home to Caxito. Would they get the beating of their life also? Or would us all venturing into Luanda be the death of us all?

"For some of us, we had to try, and out of the hundred or so women who had said they would travel, only sixteen of us actually turned up. We didn't have a loud enough voice, or so we thought. Some of the women on the streets of Luanda joined us in our march, and in our protests, women we did not know but who knew and lived our plight. There were a few women from overseas who also marched with us, and as we marched through the streets we became even stronger in numbers. Our voices were heard and we were punching the air with our fists, shouting out our message of 'NO MORE FGM! NO MORE MARITAL RAPE! OUR BODY! OUR CHOICE! SAVE OUR GIRLS! SAVE OUR FUTURE!'

"We may have started with just the fifteen of us from Caxito, but by the end of the day our numbers had swelled to more than one hundred. Small in comparison to many of the other protests, but still we had ended up with the number of women we were going to have. We were shaking with adrenalin that day, and on the journey back home we felt unstoppable. Until we reached Caxito and saw the men who terrorised us waiting for us with rage on their faces.

"The ladies who had refused to join us had been interrogated by their husbands because our husbands had started asking questions about why so many of us had gone to Luanda together that day. One beating, two beatings, three beatings and the truth came out, afraid for their lives. When the people of the town saw us dragged through the streets to be made an example of, kicked and spat on, being reminded that our men were in charge, I knew I would lose more ladies. But I couldn't stop, and I would not stop. Every time I closed my eyes I saw Mima, and I saw the visuals in my head of all of the bruises I had ever received. I would not stop, I would keep going, whether I had to go it alone or whether I had women with me. My voice would be heard and my ladies would join me again. One day, so long as I didn't give up, they would join me.

"It was the only way I could survive within myself. I could not live with myself if I gave up, and if I died trying to save these young girls and women, then I would die in the process of being the voice of women across Africa. That night I received a beating and a raping by the pastor like never before, this kind and gentle man that the local community held in such high regard. They listened to his words of wisdom in their moments of need and yet here he was a demon, the devil himself reincarnate beating the life out of his wife, the woman he had paid to take out his torment and anger on, and to unleash his masculine powers onto. This was no man, this was a monster, and if I was going to be ravaged to death, then it would be by a lion in the wilds.

"That night as I lay there with blood oozing out of my face, from the welts on my body caused by the sticks and his leather belts, and out of my vagina, I knew as soon as I could walk again, I would escape. I would walk towards Luanda, sharing with the women I met how this was not to go on. On the way to Luanda I knew I needed to stop by the hospital to have my cuts cleaned and stitched, otherwise I would not make it all the way to Luanda.

"When I did get there, no one would take me seriously. I knew that I had to have my injuries documented in some way. I had been thinking and thinking and planning this for so long and now I had the opportunity to build upon the events in Luanda a few days before. Whilst I was there, I met an angel. Would you believe I met a doctor who was visiting Africa with Doctors Without Borders, to help and assist some of the more remote hospitals, whilst researching some of the diseases and injuries we had. He was from the UK and when he saw the state I was in, he asked me to join him for a coffee. He asked me what had happened, and what had led up to this beating, and I told him everything.

"Have you seen a grown man cry? It is a shocking experience for an Angolan woman to see a man cry. But cry he did. He had so many questions and told me that one of the reasons he had chosen Central Africa was because he was a gynaecologist back in England and had seen some of the injuries and illnesses which had come from FGM. Now it was my turn to cry. I had spent months and years praying to God to send me a saviour, and it wasn't until I chose to save myself no matter what, that God answered my prayers the same night I took real actions.

"This man took photographs of my injuries, documented them thoroughly and although many of the male doctors tried to dismiss what I was telling him, he would not listen to them. He was the first man I knew to stand up for a woman and argue with the other men on behalf of the women in my country, and he wasn't even from my country.

"Once he had photographed and documented my injuries, he made some phone calls. He told me not to leave the hotel and that there would be a car coming for me. The fear within me must have been evident because he told me not to worry, they were from Doctors Without Borders and they were going to take me to the hotel where he and other doctors were staying. He then asked me if I would be willing to speak with a journalist.

"I cannot tell you how much disbelief I was in. I hadn't even made it out of my own town and here was my saviour. I sat there thinking I would be all alone for days making my way on foot to Luanda and here was a man saving me. God was saving me. I cried, and you know the scenes of the wailing hysterical women crying in gratitude? I was one of them I tell you, I was one of them.

"You see the thing is Moana, when you choose to save yourself, when you choose to save other people and you pray for help from God and the Angels, you will receive the blessings in abundance. I had almost lost my faith in God until this night. I lived with evil who spoke God's name every day to the congregation, and soon after all those years of beatings and rape you begin to lose faith in God, in humanity and in yourself.

"I was prepared to die for my cause, for my Mima, for my ladies and the future of African women, I was prepared to lose it all, and instead, here I am. All thanks to that doctor."

"What happened after you were picked up by Doctors Without Borders?" I asked her, completely unsurprised by the planning she had undertook whilst preparing to leave, and nicely surprised but not surprised by synergy which had transpired in the hospital.

I had known about Doctors Without Borders for a while, having met a couple of doctors in my own network of friends who had been part of the medical expeditions to parts of the world which needed training, supplies and doctors in abundance to help out in the civil wars and dire conditions. Many of them had worked in hospitals which they described as looking more like a town hall in a remote location, relying heavily on generators and candle light for the more serious procedures to be performed. Some of the tales had led me to Teachers Without Borders, an organisation with a similar ethos of taking education to the world, rather than medical supplies and equipment.

Alpha continued, "I was taken to Luanda in the fanciest jeep I had ever seen – a bit like the UN jeeps we had seen roll through our town but fancier – to a hotel. When I arrived, I felt so dirty and humiliated by my appearance. The lady who met me was wonderful, and she showed me to a room that had been organised for me. Her name was Lizzie, and she told me there were a few things for me in my room. *My room?* And yes there was, a table full of food and some new clothes, not to mention the biggest bathroom I had ever seen in my life. It was the size of many of the houses in our town.

"She told me that she worked with Doctors Without Borders, but was not a doctor, she was a medical journalist who travelled to different parts of the world with different doctors. She knew Pete, the doctor who had seen to my injuries and was one of the people he had called whilst sat in front of me. She told me to get a hot shower, eat something and sleep, and she would meet me for breakfast in the morning.

"I had never eaten such lovely food as I had eaten that night. It was the very best of the best of Angolan cuisine I had ever seen. The shower was the hottest and most powerful shower I had ever experienced. The bed was the comfiest and that night was the best night sleep I think I'd ever had in my life.

"I cried in the shower though, and I cried when I got into the bed too. I just couldn't believe I was being treated to all of this comfort whilst my ladies were back in their homes, living in fear of their husbands. But I had risked it all..." then she winked at me, "...for peanuts."

EIGHT

THE CHOSEN ONE

Hearing how Alpha had escaped that night from the evil of her husband to walk into a hospital and be met by a British doctor, would be to some unbelievable, but for me, I had met people in the most incredible situations that were 'just the person' I needed to meet at the time I needed to meet them. I believed in the serendipity of life, I believed in miracles, and I believed in Angels.

By the time she had finished telling me about how she had slept until the afternoon, and then eaten more than she had ever eaten in her life in one day, it was time for the boys and I to return home so I could put them both to bed.

I didn't need to put either of them to bed, I hadn't done for a while, but that night, more than any other night I wanted to. They had been part of a powerful conversation, and although it was done in a way that they could comprehend, and the word 'peanuts' had been used in the place of vagina and penis, they had learnt a lot about how life was for other people around the world; and they had told me I needed to help save the peanuts of the world and made me promise. Which I had, and now I had to connect Alpha with the names on my list, and meet her one more time, before I headed off for my life in Egypt.

We arranged to meet for another walk, but this time we took a walk around Western Park, near the various hospitals on the west side of Sheffield. It was a beautiful park with a big lake and was close to a variety of different cafes. We must have walked around the lake more than a dozen times whilst she told me of how she was taken care of by the journalists. The doctors who were in the hotel gave her a full examination and used the facilities of the Josina Machel Hospital, the oldest and largest hospital in Angola.

She told me how the doctors and journalists had shared her story internationally and locally through 'their grapevine', a term she would come to know in the years to come. Lizzie, the journalist she had met had asked her to sign disclosure documents for her to be able to document the injuries she had both internally and externally and use them in her research into FGM and what she called marital rape.

Alpha's internal injuries were documented carefully and they showed years of broken bones, scars and yet it was the injuries to her vagina that shocked the medical professionals most of all. Yes they were shocked at the amount of abuse written all over her body in injuries which had healed, but the lack of labia, clitoris and the scar tissues on her ovaries from cysts which she had once had, ones which had no doubt burst during one of her many beatings over the years.

One of the younger female Angolan doctors at the

hospital was so enraged by what she saw, she promised Alpha that she would help her in her cause to raise awareness about the dangers and abuse FGM caused to the female body. Alpha told me this young woman would become a great voice for the movement within Central Africa, not just Angola. The ladies listened to her because she was a doctor and Angolan. Little girls wanted to be her, and she not only inspired the movement of ending FGM and marital rape, but she also inspired a huge wave of educated women.

My ladies started an afternoon tea session to learn to read and write properly, and to lead their daughters by example. Some of them wanted to become teachers, and with Lizzie and Pete's support they received a group of teachers through the Teachers Without Borders movement.

Time passed both for us that day walking around the park as it did for Alpha in the hospital and back at the hotel. The journalists in the hotel had all chosen to gift Alpha a day at the spa and a hair salon, as a way of making her 'feel a million dollars' as they put it. "I had never smelled and felt so good in my life!" She laughed.

Alpha told me that when she went to sleep that night, she had cried herself to sleep at the depths of kindness everyone had bestowed upon her. She felt like the chosen one, the one God had personally chosen to go through such hardships in life so she could help other women. She felt like she was so incredibly blessed, even though she had been beaten and raped almost every day of her adult life. "To have hands move over my body so gently and carefully by the doctors and the therapists, was as if God was touching me Himself. I had never felt such tenderness. I didn't even remember the tender touch of my mother and father. I don't know if I had blocked out their touch because they had sold me to this monster, but I could never speak with them again. I was alone from the moment they sold me to that evil man."

"What happened to him? Do you know?" I asked her.

"I don't know, and I don't want to know. Rumours are rumours and some people say he told people I had lost my mind one night and gone walking off into the darkness never to return, which was true I had gone off walking never to return, but losing my mind? Quite the opposite, I had gained my mind for the first time in my life. I have heard that many of the other women knew the real story and knew I had reached Luanda and were preparing to tell the world of our plight in Angola. Others say that he was beaten by the women in the market, and was stripped of his pastor's position, and others have said he has taken a much younger wife.

"All of these stories are all word of mouth and all of them may be true in many ways. The thing to remember though is the shame he would experience. People knowing his wife had left him would be shame indeed, especially as he was a pastor. Whether he had lost his position officially, he would definitely have lost a lot of the respect of the congregation. Many of the men back home in Angola had rallied with the women and many had asked the ladies for their forgiveness for having suspected their plight but never done anything to help them.

"I spent most of my time and focus answering as many questions presented to me by the journalists as possible, and meeting with people from the British Embassy and the Asylum Seekers Council. This is when I met Jack. He was working in the embassy on a project and he arranged everything for me to leave with him in the two weeks that followed. He arranged for me to receive protection from the Angolan authorities, because at that time we were still in the throes of the civil war, and people were still unsure of who held alliances with whom. There was a huge amount of distrust within the hospital, the hotel and the embassy which is why it was rushed through so quickly.

"At first I didn't know if I wanted to leave Angola but seeing all these British people doing so much I knew that if I stayed in Angola my ladies would never stand a chance, women in Africa never stood a chance. Lizzie introduced me to another journalist, Debrah, who was getting angrier and more upset with what she was hearing from me, but like me, she knew that women needed to be the ones who stood side by side for this to stop. She was a political journalist rather than a medical journalist, so she wasn't as aware of the damage done to the female body as Lizzie was.

"Debrah had first heard of FGM when she was visiting friends in France, and there were cases of women giving birth who were having terrible problems because of the way in which the vagina had been cut when they were just small girls. She had then looked deeper into it as a social problem because many people were telling her that it was an Islaamic problem. But many of the women she had met in France were African Christians, not Muslims. It was only when she went to other districts of France that she started to meet Moroccan women who had been cut and were wanting their daughters cut. Meeting Lizzie had taken Debrah's drive to a whole new level of determination.

"Debrah was telling me how aware of the problem Europeans were becoming, and how my case would really help the west understand the situation further. When she was interviewing me she told me that my voice was going to be disguised and when her friend from Channel Four interviewed me, I would be silhouetted out, and again would have my voice changed to protect my identity. When she told me this, I cannot tell you how relieved I was, and I hadn't even considered how much I wanted to remain anonymous. I always thought I would have to show my face and when all these people at the hotel would look at me I began to realise I would be known as 'the woman who was beaten, raped and cut'. I didn't want to be that woman. I wanted to be the voice of women everywhere, but not singled out. The anonymity was the best thing for all women who went through the ordeals I had been through.

"During our conversations Debrah told me she had started in political journalism because she wanted to help women the world over who experienced domestic violence. I had never heard of either of these terms before. She told me that it wasn't the norm but it was more common than many people thought because marital rape globally was as high as 30%. To know that three in ten women were raped by their husbands shocked and upset me deeply. The control of women was a global problem due to the patriarchal system in which we all lived around the world, and women were rising up in a lot of different ways.

"Women were fighting for their right to have managerial jobs, they were fighting for equal pay, they were fighting for the right to homeschool their children, and a whole host of other things they had been denied. I didn't understand why these women wanted to homeschool their children when people in Africa were wanting to be able to have a school to send their children to, and I knew I had a lot to learn about life in England. Both Jack and Debrah spent the next two weeks talking with me about what to expect when I arrived and how I would be helped with housing and given some money to buy more clothes, and I remember thinking what a strange thing this was.

"Why would England, and all these people I had just met want to help me so much? Why would I be given a home when I was not English? Why would these people help me? And I realised that it is what good people do. In my hometown of Caxita, we would help each other with the farming, and if one of our ladies hadn't got enough food or needed help with the children, we would help each other. This was no different, it was still a community helping a member of the community. It didn't matter that I was black, or that I was a woman from Africa. These people did what they were doing because it was the right thing to do.

"The days leading up to me leaving for England I was very nervous. I had never seen an aeroplane other than in the sky, and here I was about to board one for my new life in England. Jack told me what it would feel like as we took off, and he told me that my ears may 'pop'. I didn't understand what he meant until we had a drink of coffee on the plane and I swallowed. I hadn't realised that I could not hear that well either.

"Jack told me that it was unheard of for the British Government to rush through such a case as quickly as they had, and it had only happened due to the extent of my injuries and because there was such international pressure on countries helping those in the various civil wars across Africa. He told me what he knew about the conflict diamonds, and how even though America, South Africa, the Soviet Union and Cuba were involved, Britain had tried to remain out of it 'to remain impartial' but they just could not ignore my situation. And as I had already met with so many journalists, there would be international speculation as to why they had not helped me. He told me, 'Make no mistake Alpha, they are doing this as much for themselves, if not more so than they are for you. You are like a golden ticket, the chosen one for British politicians to look good in all of this'.

"I was glad he told me that, and yet I felt like the chosen one for so many different reasons. I felt like God had chosen me; that I had chosen me; and even though my ladies had been left behind to deal with their life in their own way, I felt that them attending all my afternoon teas, they had chosen me. And I knew I would not let my ladies down.

"What I wasn't expecting though was the amount of kindness I would receive when I finally did arrive in Heathrow. Jack and I were met by a lady called Sarah and another man called Derek, and they both told me, 'Welcome to England, Alpha. We hope you will like it here'.

"I couldn't stop looking around me at how clean and organised everything was. All the shops looked clean and inviting, and all the ladies dressed so beautifully. Being hugged, kissed, and looked at with love by their husbands. Their men taking their luggage from them, and putting their arms through each other, holding hands. It was like the dream us ladies back in Africa had believed would come true for us, but it never did.

"All the cars I saw looked brand new, and even the ones which were old, still looked brand new. I knew I was in a different world, not just a different country. Sitting in the back of the car looking out of the window, I thought back to how Africa had been raped by the men at war, just like the women were raped every night in their bed by the men they had married. To be African meant to be raped was the conclusion I came to in my mind on that long drive. They raped our land for oil and diamonds; they raped our communities for money so they did not have to pay for their lavish lifestyles in Luanda; they raped our families of our children, the boys off to fight in a senseless war, and our girls to be sold off to the highest bidder; they raped us, the women who toiled the land and fed the community.

"At one point I thought to myself, *African men are evil*. Then I had to remember that many of them did not choose the life, they were taught the life. They were young boys, our sons, when the military came and put guns in their hands, sometimes when they were as young as nine. It was all they knew, violence. Kill or be killed. Take or be taken. I cried so many times on that journey Moana, I don't mind telling you I cried, and Sarah asked me several times if I needed to stop and have a cup of tea. I learnt on that trip that tea was the answer for being upset.

"We did stop and have a cup of tea, and I spoke with Sarah about what was going through my mind. Jack, Sarah and Derek sat and listened. Derek had to get up and walk away. He later told me that just hearing what I had shared, what Debrah and Lizzie had told him about my story and liaising with Jack on bringing me home, he felt both guilt and shame, and a sense of inadequacy as a man because he knew there was nothing he could do to take away my pain. I was confused by this, why would he need to take away my pain? I wasn't his daughter, sister or his wife. I had a lot to learn about what good men felt and the way they thought about things.

"We had been on a road which I now know very well, the M1, and Jack told me there was someone on the phone for me. I looked at him and then looked at this thing he was handing to me. I had never seen a mobile phone before, let alone used one. I said 'Hello' into the part he showed me and held the other end to my ear, and on the line was Debrah all the way from Angola. I couldn't believe it Moana. I was talking with someone in Africa and I was in England. How could this possibly be happening?

"Jack was smiling to himself at the look of confusion on my face and when Debrah told me the news that my interview with Channel Four had been scheduled for release in a couple of weeks, and that the story she had written about me would be featured in the newspapers in the next couple of days, I didn't quite understand what she meant. How could I be in the newspaper and on this channel called Channel Four, a channel I had never heard of.

"We had never had a television in Caxita, it wasn't something that a home ever had. Some of the nicer hotels where the pastor had taken me to meet with his fellow businessmen had televisions, but not like I had seen in the cafes as we walked through the airport. I hadn't just left my home country, as far away from the pastor as possible, but I had entered a different world all together.

"I remember looking out of the window on the way here to Sheffield thinking about how green it was and how it reminded me of a lot of the fields back home after the rainy season. I started to cry silent tears because here I was on the other side of the world and my ladies were still home, still being beaten, still being raped, still having their daughters sold to the highest bidder as soon as their monthly bleeds were happening, promised to them by the man who I had shared my life with.

"One of the things Debrah and Jack asked me whilst I was back in Angola was how could they best help me and my ladies, and I had told them about all the ideas we'd had about creating the leaflets and yet had very few resources to make them in large numbers. They said they would help, and would reach out to people they knew around the world where all of this was happening. They would help me and my ladies. I cried at their kindness. I think I cried more happy tears in those few weeks than I have ever cried. And still the kindness kept coming.

"When we reached the place which was to be my home for the weeks to come whilst they 'sorted something more permanent out for me' I met other ladies from all over

Africa, all over England, people who were Muslims, Christians, didn't believe or know what to believe, young, and old. Here we all were in this home for women, hiding from the men who we had married. We were slow to share our stories and yet some of these women are still very good friends of mine today.

"After a week in my new home, I received a letter addressed directly to me. I still have it in my home. Do you know what it was?"

"No, tell me, what was it," I replied.

"Well, I knew they must have been very connected to help things move so quickly in getting me out of Angola, but what I didn't know was just how well connected Jack and Debrah were. Inside this envelope was one of the first leaflets for me and my ladies. When I saw the leaflet it had the UN logo on it, the Asylum Seekers Council logo on it, Doctors Without Borders and Teachers Without Borders, and many more besides. I was overcome with emotion, I wailed and dropped to my knees. I was laughing and crying all at the same time. There was a map of Angola on the back, next to all the countries where FGM had the highest numbers: Sierra Leone, Morocco, Egypt, Ethiopia, and Cameroon all highlighted. And on the front was my silhouette, no name, no country but I knew it was me. It was every African woman. It was the first piece of literature I saw created for my cause, my ladies, for all of us ladies. It was real Moana, and everything I had been planning whilst preparing to leave that night, was real.

"I still have nightmares of those times back in Africa, and my ladies are in my prayers every night. I pray they are safe; I pray they have had the courage to leave like I did, and I pray they have not been murdered by the monsters they call husbands.

"I know with the work Debrah, Jack, Sarah, Derek, Anwar, and I have done over the last few years is making a difference to the lives of women around the world. I have been chosen to speak at what they call closed events, I have been interviewed more times than I can remember about what happened to me and my ladies back home in Angola, and each time I share my story, share the story of all of us women who are brutalised by the men, the traditions and the cultures of our past, I get stronger. I become more determined by the moment.

"I don't know how you will help us; I know you have a list of names you can give me, and I know the introductions you make will always bear fruit. I have seen you speak, I have read your articles. So even if you email me from Egypt with your findings, and you introduce me to organisations you discover there, or send me articles to publish? Maybe you may even share this in a book one day, because you will write books, you have to, your writing and observations of the world we live in are too important not to share with the world. Whatever you do, I hope you never forget me and my ladies. Promise me, you will never forget us, and that you will share our story."

"I promise I will share your story one day, but I have a question for you," I said.

"Yes, what is it?" Alpha asked.

"How on God's earth do you believe you are a woman that anyone can forget?"

With that she laughed her beautiful laugh, threw her head back, and then threw her arms around me, and it was in that moment that we both cried our eyes out. In part knowing this would probably be the very last time we saw each other, and in part because the journey we had shared over these past few weeks had been intense, even with a dose of peanuts.

CLITERATURE

It wasn't until I had moved to Egypt that I was sent an article by a friend back in the UK, and saw Alpha's name in print. I looked her up and saw a plethora of articles, leaflets and interviews she had done. She had come out of the shadows and she had put her face and her name to the cause. I cried tears of joy and sat there with my head in my hands at the dining table.

The boys came over and asked me if I was okay. I told them, "Yes boys, I am more than okay."

"So why are you crying then?" asked Salah.

Marai took a look at my laptop and with a big smile on his face said, "This is why Salah."

"Hey, that's Aunty Alpha! She did it! She's telling everyone about her peanuts being taken away." He jumped up and down dancing around the room saying, "Go Aunty Peanuts! I mean, Aunty Alpha!" He threw himself on the floor laughing. "Aunty Peanuts! Haha that is so funny."

"So what does this mean now, Mummy?" Marai asked me.

"Well, I am going to email this to a few people I have met here and show them what Aunty Alpha has been up to, and see if they can help," I replied.

"And I will make you tea, Mummy," Marai said as he gave me a big hug.

"Thank you Baaba, that would be lovely."

I was incredibly proud of her and the work her, Jack and Anwar had done together. The level of involvement, and the introductions I knew Jack had made, must have been pivotal. I sent all of them an email telling them what I had just received, how I had seen Alpha in the media, and congratulated them on all they had done towards putting FGM in the mainstream media.

Alpha had spoken in the House of Commons, been interviewed by some of the biggest names in politics, created so many more leaflets she had wanted to create with her ladies, and she had created links all over the world with the work that she was doing.

Connecting her to the names I had promised and seeing photos of them together on stages on the various websites to do with FGM, domestic abuse and human rights demonstrations made me so grateful to have been part of her journey, even though it had only been in connecting a few dots here and there. She had followed them up, had done the work, and she had connected the dots.

The woman she had become, and the way her name resonated around the world was a force to be reckoned with when it came to FGM. She had inspired many more names to come to light. Movies were being made, documentaries have since been made and her involvement in the consultation process I know will have her crying those happy tears she cried when she first went to sleep that night in Luanda, Angola, in the big fancy hotel.

Angola may be out of the civil war, conflict diamonds may not be needed to fund the war as they once were, but they are still a problem in the region. Probably always will be. Angolan's may now have some kind of independence, but there is still a way to go, and the practice of FGM is receiving more and more exposure than ever before. It is becoming illegal in many countries, and the sex trafficking and child bride selection process is coming to light in ways unheard of before.

Much of the work that is being done around the world is due to the bravery of women like Alpha. There isn't just one voice, and I understood why Alpha had wanted to be anonymous at the beginning. If she had been the face, it would have pigeon holed her and the entire story as an Angolan one.

Women are taking a stand for each other. Men are taking a stand for the women they love, the sons, the brothers, the husbands and the friends. Families are not being raped for war or for control anymore in the numbers they once were. More and more people have access to mobile phones, even if they do not have access to education and clothes. Due to refurbished mobile phones being shipped around the world, and the access to the internet becoming cheaper every day, the world is becoming smaller as more and more countries are going online. Atrocities, corruption, poverty and abuses from what were once considered remote are now being spread by the videos individuals share via social media networks.

The more we all connect the dots, the more we share our stories, the more we are willing to open ourselves up to the world, and the more we stop learning about things in order to simply speak of them at dinner parties, the sooner we will be able to support more and more women like Alpha and her ladies. The problems of the world will one day reach our shores, either through immigration, the news or our social media platforms as we travel the world and share what we see, learn and experience. Many may not like 'the immigrants' arriving in their country but it is important to understand why the immigrants arrive and what part our country had in bringing their troubles to their door.

We also have to ask ourselves: what would we do if we were them? Where would we go? Would we stay and perish, or would we, like Alpha, make a run for it? Alpha was one of the lucky ones, she didn't have to go far to find help. Many people have to cross borders and risk their lives crossing oceans in small boats.

Alpha never returned to Angola, she couldn't, but she was able to find her ladies, the ones who survived the violence at the hands of the men who they called husbands.

The 'cliterature' created by Alpha, the doctors in the hospital in Caxito, Jack, Lizzie and Debrah, and the other journalists in their network, reached the town of Caxito, and Alpha's ladies knew it was her who had gotten out alive. Debrah had delivered the leaflets herself to a list of names given to her by Alpha. Upon seeing the leaflets many of the ladies cheered Alpha's name in the streets. Many of them danced in celebration that she was still alive. And many of them fell to the floor in relief that their friend, their sister, their leader had made it out of Africa alive.

Alpha had given them all a new surge of courage, a new wave of strength and many of Alpha's ladies now speak out in a free Angola about the abuse they have experienced. Many of the men have been arrested and many of the doctors, businessmen and pastors involved in the sex trafficking have been detained indefinitely due to the testimonies of these ladies.

Alpha's project of education is now seen on websites, in places of worship, in hospitals, medical schools, and in university lectures and high schools across the world. FGM is now on the lips of women and men around the world, and the vaginas of the women around the world are becoming safer.

One of the things I told Alpha I would love to see is reconstructive surgery being done for many of these women around the world who have been so brutalised at the hands of men and women who have not had proper medical training – not because of them being able to feel pure pleasure down there – but so they can survive childbirth. This too was one of her hopes and dreams, because one of the highest rates of women dying in childbirth in African countries is due to the mutilated vaginas in which they have to push a baby through. The deaths of young girls due to the internal bleeding, the infections, the cysts, and suicide make for horrendous reading, and yet read about it we must.

What we are seeing is not just Alpha's story, it is the story of women around the world, and it is not until we all join forces and speak up for ourselves and others that we can put a stop to the tyranny of our sisters around the world.

The amount of cliterature around the world has been mainly focused on erotica, the use of pleasure from vibrators and women who have a whole and complete vagina. All our vaginas are sacred, all our vaginas are worthy of pleasure, and all our vaginas need to be written about, whether they are whole and complete, or whether they have been mutilated.

Thankfully, due to Alpha and women like her, we are now seeing the increase in information shared about the truths of FGM – that it is NOT a religious practice, that it isn't just an Asian, African or a Muslim thing. It is a global practice aimed at chaste women and their sexuality for centuries, across social classes, across nations and ethnicities. Only when we stop seeing it as a foreign practice, an Islaamic problem and a problem which belongs to others, and start seeing it for what it is, then women can truly be liberated. And the great thing about that is, that the men will be even more satisfied, the vibration of the planet will be elevated and people will come together in more ways than one.

Rape within marriage is also not an African problem, nor is it a Muslim problem. It is a human problem. When we speak openly about our suffering, when we report those who rape us to the authorities, even to our doctors, men and women – because women are not the only victims of rape within marriage, or out of it – when we report these abuses, we grow in strength, we teach our children that the abuse is not acceptable, that we are not victims, that we have the right to say NO. Our bodies are ours; they are not for others to do with as they wish, they are not for others to tell us what to do and what not to do with.

Our bodies, our choices.

Regardless of what our choices are, we have to make our voices heard. We have to give a voice to the voiceless, a louder voice to those screaming to be heard, because all our futures depend upon it, maybe not today, maybe not in our lifetime, but the choices we make today will impact our children and our children's children.

The ripple effect of our actions will reach far and wide, and we will never know the lives we save. Alpha had no idea what would happen the night she ran from the pastor. She had no idea that just trusting her intuition to run, to leave, and to speak out, all this would happen. Alpha believed what was happening was wrong, that she and her ladies deserved more, and she trusted that belief.

This is why I have chosen to share Alpha's story, and this is why I do the work I do. It may not be easy work to do, it may not be an easy read, but read and know about it we must.

The recommendation of this book, and the others in *The Sacral Series*, will all make a difference, so please share them with others, let people know what you learn, and remember, these may be written with false names and a different location and ethnicity to the person who shared their story with me, but the facts of the nations, ethnicities and faiths, are all correct. The conversations and interactions you read are true, everything you read is true, the only reason the names, locations and identities are changed, is to protect the person who's story it is and their families.

Thank you for reading, thank you for caring enough to want to learn more, and thank you for being the next voice in the world of change.

We need your help, humanity needs your help, and not just with the issues in this book, but in all the books in this series.

Alpha healed herself through fighting for social justice for her nation. She channelled her pain, her anger and her fear into being the voice of change, and you can too. Whatever you are experiencing, if you know you deserve better, if you need help, reach out, get help.

Be strong. Be brave always. One step, one night, one whisper at a time.

With love and gratitude always,
Moana x

GRATITUDE

First of all, thank you to Alpha for sharing your story with me all those years ago. The courage, the smiles and the tears in which you worked through inspired me in more ways than you will ever know. Knowing your story, being trusted with your story in the hope that one day I would share it was an honour I didn't know what to do with. I can only pray that I have done your story, the story of over 200 million women worldwide, justice.

To Jerry Lampson for the incredible interpretation of the brief in designing this front cover, one that as you said "you'll either love it or hate it". I loved it from the very moment I saw it, and – with a few tweaks here and there – you nailed it, as you always do. I am so blessed to have you by my side as a friend, my designer and my voice of reason and focus. Thank you for being in my life, for being patient and for being you.

I am grateful to Adam R. Walton, my friend and co-host of The Sacral Series Podcasts which accompany all the books in the series, for holding space for me in the conversations which need to be had, and for asking pertinent questions in those conversations. These are not easy conversations to have, and it takes a lot of courage and integrity to a higher purpose to have them. Thank you for walking this path with me, for being my friend and for being the man you are.

This book wouldn't be available to any of you if it weren't for the incredible talents of my right hand woman Linda Diggle keeping me focused when I purge the trauma of these stories into the porcelain. Knowing that I can turn to you whilst crying my eyes out and needing tea as I purge these stories in this series is such a gift. No words I write about how grateful I am for you and to you would ever be enough. I love you. So much, but then you know that already.

To my mum and dad, as always I thank you for keeping me grounded and encouraging me in all I do, for being my parents and for giving me the solid foundations upon which to build. You may not have liked having to shout at me to get my head out of a "bloody book" when I was younger, but to have your words of "you better get writing your next one" means more than you will ever know. Thank you for being there as I purge these stories and for reminding me to "just get on with it" when I feel at a loss on what to do next.

To Khaalid and Naasir, two incredible humans who I'm so honoured to call my sons. To be your mother is the greatest gift I could ever have asked, and to have you keep me grounded with words of "Yeah it's alright" and "Not too shabby" and asking "What's next then?" keeps me focused, driven and humble. Without you both by my side in all the ways you are, even though we are thousands of miles apart, none of the work I do in this world would make sense. You are my air on so many occasions, my driving force and my inspiration. I love you with every fibre of my being, and remember always use your voice, because what you think, feel and dream of is so important.

And finally to you, the person reading this book. THANK YOU for choosing to be open to the subject matter, for having the courage to pick up the book and read it. That in and of itself is a courageous act. I honour you, because even by reading this book you are playing a small part in helping to bring these atrocities to an end.

With love to you all,
Dawn

ABOUT HAJAH KANDEH

Hajah Kandeh fled the conflict diamond war in her country of birth, Sierra Leone, where she had suffered tremendous violence. She credits her survival to all the strangers who have "loved her into being".

At 16, she won a scholarship to France after placing first in the national exams for best French language students. In college she won a "Best Actress" award for *The Revelation*, a play she wrote and starred in. She graduated First Class from Fourah Bay College, University of Sierra Leone where she majored in Political Science and French literature.

After college, she worked for the BBC as a freelance writer in Sierra Leone. Upon arriving in San Francisco, she struggled to establish herself in her new home working retail, customer service, nannying, and other jobs most immigrants do to get started in America. After working in the hospitality department of Saks, and later getting her certification, she secured a position as a mental health counsellor for a local non-profit.

She actively engages in women's writing groups and conferences, including "Writing Ourselves Whole," where women of all backgrounds come together and connect through writing and telling their stories.

Hajah loves poetry, smart movies and great

conversations. She has been afraid of snakes most of her life. She is fluent in several languages including French, Russian, and Krio and dreams of traveling the world some day.

She is the founder of Do Tell, an organisation which aims to educate and empower children to speak up in a safe space about sexual abuse and other forms of violation. Her passion is to help them through the long journey of healing necessary to becoming healthy whole adults capable of living fulfilling lives.

Hajah lives in San Francisco with her son and a feisty black cat named Luna where she pays it forward by making magic wherever she goes, one person at a time, one day at a time.

ABOUT DAWN BATES

Dawn is best known for her profound wisdom, truth slaying and high energy, not to mention a trademark giggle.

An international bestselling author multiple times over, author coach, business strategist, and publisher, Dawn specialises in developing global step change and brand expansion strategies, underpinned with powerful leadership and profound truths.

She writes for various magazines, and when not sailing around the world on yachts, writing countless books, or studying for her PhD in International Law and Social Justice, she appears on various media channels highlighting and discussing important subjects in today's society. She is also the host of *The Truth Serum* podcast launched in 2021.

All her books are powerful, bringing together the multi-faceted aspects of the world we live in and taking you on rollercoaster rides of emotions, whilst delivering mic dropping inspiration, motivation and awakening. Her body of work captures life around the world in all its rawness.

Dawn's expertise lies in making you rethink your life, whilst harnessing the deepest freedom of all: your own truth.

She's an authority on leading others to create exceptional results by igniting the passions and fire deep within and shifting them from fear, feelings of imposter and self-doubt to living life where they are free to speak and live powerfully.

To discover more about Dawn, connect with her on the various social media platforms:

- facebook.com/realdawnbates
- twitter.com/realdawnbates
- instagram.com/realdawnbates
- linkedin.com/in/dawnbates

If you have purchased a copy of this book, I would love for you to send me a selfie of you and my book.

Tag me on:

facebook.com/RealDawnBates

instagram.com/realdawnbates

twitter.com/realdawnbates

linkedin.com/in/dawnbates

…so I can thank you in person.

Ciao for now mi amore, and be blessed always x

www.ingramcontent.com/pod-product-compliance
Lightning Source LLC
Chambersburg PA
CBHW021441080526
44588CB00009B/632